# The Life and Teachings of Thoth Hermes Trismegistus

*Ancient Wisdom on Divinity, Transformation, and the Cosmos*

## A Modern Translation

Adapted for the Contemporary Reader

## Hermes Trismegistus

# Table of Contents

# Preface - Message to the Reader

**Rebuilding the Greatest Library in Human History**

Thousands of years ago, the Library of Alexandria was the heart of global knowledge — a sanctuary where the wisdom of every known civilization was gathered and shared freely.

And then, it was lost.

Now, we're rebuilding it — and you are invited to join us.

At the Library of Alexandria, we've set out to make every book available to *every person on Earth* — not just in print, but in every language, every format, and for every reader.

Here's how we do it:

- **Deluxe Print Editions at True Printing Cost** - Order any book as a high-quality paperback, elegant hardcover, or stunning boxset — and only pay what it costs to print. No markups. No middlemen.

- **Unlimited Access to the Greatest Works** - Enjoy thousands of timeless classics — from Plato to Shakespeare to Tolstoy — in beautiful, modern eBook and audiobook editions. Read and listen without limits — for every reader, everywhere.

- **Modern Translations for Every Language & Dialect** - We're reimagining the classics in clear, accessible language — and translating them into every dialect imaginable. Everyone deserves to understand humanity's greatest ideas.

When you visit **LibraryofAlexandria.com**, you're not just accessing books — you're joining a global movement to restore, preserve, and share the wisdom of civilization.

**Join us today at LibraryofAlexandria.com**

Together, we'll ensure the light of human wisdom never fades again.

With gratitude,
**The Modern Library of Alexandria Team**

**Visit:**

**www.libraryofalexandria.com**

**Or scan the code below:**

# The Life and Teachings of Thoth Hermes Trismegistus

*THUNDER boomed, and lightning lit up the sky. The veil hanging in the Temple was torn from top to bottom. The wise initiator, dressed in robes of blue and gold, slowly lifted his jeweled staff and pointed it toward the darkness that had been revealed behind the torn silk curtain. "Behold the Light of Egypt!" he declared.*

*The candidate, dressed in a simple white robe, stared into the deep blackness framed between two massive columns topped with lotus flowers, where the veil had once hung. As he stood there, a soft, glowing mist began to spread throughout the air until the atmosphere shimmered with tiny glowing particles. The candidate's face lit up from the soft glow, and he scanned the glittering mist, hoping to spot something solid within it.*

*The initiator spoke again: "This Light you see is the hidden radiance of the Mysteries. No one knows where it comes from, except for the 'Master of the Light.' Behold Him!"*

Suddenly, through the glowing haze, a figure emerged, surrounded by a flickering greenish light. The initiator lowered his staff, bowed his head humbly, and placed one hand flat against his chest in reverence.

The candidate took a step back, overwhelmed and partially blinded by the brilliance of the figure before him. Slowly, he gathered his courage and looked again at the Divine One. The figure was much larger than any human being, and its body was partly transparent, revealing a glowing heart and brain that pulsed with radiant energy.

As the candidate watched in amazement, the heart of the figure transformed into an ibis, while the brain became a shining emerald. The mysterious being held in its hand a winged staff coiled with serpents.

The aged initiator lifted his staff again and cried out in a booming voice: "All hail to you, Thoth Hermes, Thrice Greatest! All hail, Prince of Men! All hail to you who stand upon the head of Typhon!"

At that moment, a terrifying dragon appeared—a monstrous creature that was part serpent, part crocodile, and part hog. Flames burst from its mouth and nostrils, and horrible sounds echoed throughout the chamber.

Without hesitation, Hermes struck the advancing dragon with his serpent-twined staff. With a snarling cry, the beast collapsed onto its side, and the flames around it slowly faded.

*Hermes placed his foot firmly on the skull of the defeated Typhon. In the next instant, a burst of unbearable light filled the room, forcing the candidate to stumble back against one of the pillars.*

*Streams of greenish mist trailed behind Hermes as he moved across the chamber, and with a final flash, the immortal figure vanished into nothingness.*

• • •

# Suppositions Concerning
# The Identity of Hermes

Iamblichus claimed that Hermes wrote twenty thousand books, while Manetho said the number was more than thirty-six thousand (see James Gardner). These numbers make it clear that a single person, even if gifted with divine abilities, could hardly have created so many works alone. It is said that Hermes revealed many arts and sciences to humanity, including medicine, chemistry, law, art, astrology, music, rhetoric, magic, philosophy, geography, mathematics (especially geometry), anatomy, and public speaking. Orpheus was honored in a similar way by the Greeks.

In his *Biographia Antiqua*, Francis Barrett writes about Hermes: "* * * if God ever appeared in a man, he appeared in him, as is shown by his books and his *Pymander*. In these works, Hermes shared the secrets of the Abyss and divine knowledge with future generations. Through them, he proved himself to be not only an inspired prophet but also a profound philosopher, gaining his wisdom from God and the heavens, not from humans."

Because of his great knowledge, Hermes was connected with many ancient sages and prophets. In *Ancient Mythology*, Bryant says: "I have mentioned that Cadmus was the same as the Egyptian Thoth; it is clear from his identification as Hermes, and from the fact that he was credited with inventing writing." (The chapter on Pythagorean Mathematics includes a table of the original Cadmean letters.) Scholars believe that Hermes was known to the Jews as "Enoch," whom Kenealy called the "Second Messenger of God."

The Greeks accepted Hermes into their mythology, and he later became known as Mercury among the Romans. He was honored through the planet Mercury because it is the closest to the Sun. Just as Mercury orbits near the Sun, Hermes was thought to be closest to God and became known as the Messenger of the Gods.

In Egyptian drawings, Thoth, identified as Hermes, is shown carrying a wax writing tablet and recording the weighing of souls in the judgment hall of Osiris—a ritual of deep meaning. Hermes is especially important to Masonic scholars because he is believed to have created the Masonic initiation rituals, which were based on the Mysteries he established. Most of the symbols used in Masonry are Hermetic in nature. Pythagoras studied mathematics with the Egyptians and learned about symbolic geometric shapes from them.

Hermes is also remembered for reforming the calendar by increasing the year from 360 days to 365, setting a standard that we still use today. The title "Thrice Greatest" was given to Hermes because he was considered the greatest philosopher, the greatest

priest, and the greatest king. Notably, the final poem written by
Henry Wadsworth Longfellow, one of America's beloved poets,
was a lyrical ode to Hermes. (See *Chambers' Encyclopædia*.)

...

# The Mutilated Hermetic Fragments

James Campbell Brown, in his *History of Chemistry*, writes about the Hermetic books: "Leaving behind the Chaldean and earliest Egyptian times, from which we have only remnants and no records—no names of chemists or philosophers—we now move into the historical period, when books were first written, not on parchment or paper, but on papyrus. A collection of early Egyptian books is credited to Hermes Trismegistus, who may have been a real scholar or perhaps a symbol for many different authors over time. * * * Some connect him with the Greek god Hermes, as well as with the Egyptian god Thoth or Tuti, who was the moon god, often shown in art with the head of an ibis and the disc and crescent of the moon. The Egyptians saw him as the god of wisdom, writing, and timekeeping.

Because of the high regard alchemists had for Hermes, chemical writings became known as 'hermetic,' and the term 'hermetically sealed'—used to describe sealing a glass container by melting it shut—comes from this tradition. The same origin can be found in Paracelsus' hermetic medicines and the hermetic freemasonry of the Middle Ages."

Among the fragments believed to come from Hermes are two famous works. One is the *Emerald Tablet*, and the other is the *Divine Pymander*, also called *The Shepherd of Men*, which will be discussed later. Hermes stands out as one of the few pagan philosophers whom the early Christians did not attack. In fact, some Church Fathers even admitted that Hermes showed signs of intelligence. They said that if he had lived in a more enlightened age and had received their teachings, he could have been truly great.

In *Stromata*, Clement of Alexandria, one of the few ancient writers whose accounts of pagan traditions survive today, shares nearly all we know about the original forty-two books of Hermes and how highly they were valued by both the spiritual and political leaders of Egypt. Clement describes a ceremonial procession like this:

"For the Egyptians follow their own philosophy, which is reflected in their rituals. First comes the Singer, holding a symbol of music. He must study two of Hermes' books: one containing hymns to the gods and another with rules for the king's life. Following the Singer is the Astrologer, carrying a clock and a palm branch—both symbols of astrology. He must memorize four books of Hermes about the stars: one on the fixed stars, another on the phases of the sun and moon, and the other two on their risings.

Next in the procession is the sacred Scribe, wearing wings on his head and carrying a book and measuring tool, along with ink and a reed for writing. He must know the hieroglyphs and be familiar with cosmography, geography, the paths of the sun and moon, the five planets, and the layout of Egypt, including a chart of the Nile.

He also needs to understand the priests' equipment, sacred spaces, and rituals. After the Scribe comes the Stole-keeper, carrying the cubit of justice and a ceremonial cup for offerings. He is skilled in matters of training and sacrifice.

There are ten books dedicated to the worship of the gods, covering topics like sacrifices, hymns, prayers, processions, and festivals. Lastly comes the Prophet, holding a water vase, with followers carrying bread behind him. As the temple leader, the Prophet studies ten more books called 'Hieratic,' which contain laws, knowledge of the gods, and priestly training. The Prophet also manages the temple's resources. Of Hermes' forty-two essential books, thirty-six contain Egyptian philosophy, studied by the individuals mentioned above. The remaining six books, which are medical, are entrusted to the Pastophoroi, or image-bearers, and deal with anatomy, diseases, medical tools, treatments, eye care, and women's health."

One of the greatest losses to philosophy was the destruction of nearly all these forty-two books of Hermes. They disappeared during the burning of Alexandria. Both the Romans and later the Christians understood that as long as these books existed, they could not fully dominate the Egyptian people. The few volumes that escaped the fire were hidden in the desert, and only a small group of initiates from secret schools know where they are buried.

• • •

# The Book of Thoth

While Hermes still walked among men, he entrusted the sacred *Book of Thoth* to his chosen successors. This book contained the secret methods for bringing about the spiritual rebirth of humanity and served as the key to understanding all of Hermes' other writings. Although the exact contents of the *Book of Thoth* are unknown, it is said that the pages were filled with strange hieroglyphs and symbols. Those who knew how to use them gained unlimited power over the spirits of the air and the gods beneath the earth.

The book also revealed the process by which certain areas of the brain could be stimulated through the Mysteries, expanding human consciousness. This allowed individuals to see the Immortals and stand in the presence of higher gods. Because it described how this awakening could be achieved, the *Book of Thoth* was known as the "Key to Immortality."

According to legend, the *Book of Thoth* was kept inside a golden box in the inner sanctuary of a temple. Only one key existed, held by the "Master of the Mysteries," the highest Hermetic initiate. He alone knew what was written in the book. When the Mysteries faded from the ancient world, the book was lost.

However, devoted followers carried the sealed casket to another land. It is believed that the book still exists today, guiding those who seek the presence of the Immortals. No further details about the book can be revealed to the world now, but the unbroken line of initiation—starting with the first hierophant initiated by Hermes—continues to this day. Those who are truly dedicated to serving the Immortals may find this priceless work if they search with sincerity and determination.

Some claim that the *Book of Thoth* is, in fact, the mysterious Tarot of the Bohemians—a symbolic collection of seventy-eight cards, said to have been carried by the gypsies since they were exiled from their ancient temple, the Serapeum. (According to secret histories, the gypsies were originally priests from Egypt.) There are still several secret schools in the world today that initiate worthy students into the Mysteries. Almost all of them began by lighting their sacred flames from the torch of Hermes.

In the *Book of Thoth*, Hermes revealed the "One Way" to humanity. For centuries, the wise from every culture and faith have followed this path to reach immortality. Hermes created this Way to shine a light in the darkness, offering redemption to humankind.

• • •

# Poimandres, The
# Vision of Hermes

The *Divine Pymander* of Hermes Mercurius Trismegistus is one of the earliest surviving Hermetic writings. Although it likely does not exist in its original form—having been reworked during the first centuries of the Christian era and mistranslated over time—it still holds many core ideas of the Hermetic tradition. The *Divine Pymander* is made up of seventeen fragments, gathered and presented as one complete work. The second book, called *Poimandres* or *The Vision*, describes how divine wisdom was first revealed to Hermes. After receiving this knowledge, Hermes began his ministry, teaching the secrets of the unseen universe to anyone willing to listen.

*The Vision* is the most well-known Hermetic fragment and explains the Hermetic view of the universe and the Egyptian teachings on how the human soul develops and grows. For some time, it was mistakenly called *The Genesis of Enoch*, but this error has since been corrected. To interpret the symbolic meaning in Hermes' *Vision*, the following works were used: *The Divine Pymander* (London, 1650), translated from Arabic and Greek by Dr. Everard; *Hermetica* (Oxford, 1924), edited by Walter Scott;

*Hermes, The Mysteries of Egypt* (Philadelphia, 1925), by Edouard Schuré; and *Thrice-Greatest Hermes* (London, 1906), by G. R. S. Mead. These sources were supplemented with commentary based on the ancient Egyptian esoteric philosophy and other Hermetic writings. Outdated language has been replaced with modern terms, and the narrative style has been chosen over the original dialogue format for clarity.

While wandering through a barren, rocky landscape, Hermes devoted himself to meditation and prayer. By following the secret teachings of the Temple, he gradually freed his higher mind from the control of his bodily senses. Once released, his divine nature revealed to him the mysteries of the spiritual realms. He saw a figure of immense power and awe—a Great Dragon whose wings stretched across the sky, with light radiating from its body in all directions. (In the Mysteries, the Universal Life Force is symbolized by a dragon.) The Dragon called Hermes by name and asked him why he was contemplating the World Mystery. Overwhelmed with fear, Hermes bowed before the Dragon and begged to know its identity.

The Dragon responded that it was Poimandres, the Mind of the Universe, the Creative Intelligence, and the supreme ruler of all things. (According to Schuré, Poimandres represents the god Osiris.) Hermes asked Poimandres to reveal the structure of the universe and the nature of the gods. The Dragon agreed, telling Hermes to hold its image firmly in his mind.

At that moment, Poimandres' form changed into a brilliant, pulsing light. This light was the true spiritual essence of the Great Dragon. Hermes was lifted into the heart of this radiant glow, and the material world vanished from his awareness. Then a deep darkness descended, spreading out until it completely swallowed the light. Chaos followed, and a swirling, watery substance emerged, releasing clouds of vapor. Strange sounds filled the air, moaning and sighing, as though the light trapped within the darkness was crying out. Hermes realized that the light represented the spiritual universe, while the swirling darkness symbolized material substance.

From the light trapped in the darkness came a mysterious and sacred Word, which stood upon the smoky waters. This Word—known as the Voice of the Light—rose from the darkness like a mighty pillar. Fire and air followed the Word upward, while earth and water remained below. In this way, the waters of light were separated from the waters of darkness. The upper waters formed the worlds above, while the lower waters created the worlds below. Earth and water mixed together and became inseparable, and the Spiritual Word, called Reason, moved over their surface, stirring it into motion.

Then Poimandres spoke again, though he did not reveal his form: "I, your God, am the Light and the Mind that existed before spirit and matter were separated, before darkness and light were divided. The Word, which appeared as a pillar of flame, is the Son of God, born from the mystery of the Mind. Its name is Reason. Reason is the child of Thought, and it will divide light from darkness, placing Truth in the midst of the waters. Understand this, Hermes, and reflect deeply upon it. What sees and hears within you is not of the earth—it is the Word of God living within you. This is why it is said that divine light exists even within mortal darkness, and ignorance cannot divide them. The union of the Word and the Mind creates the mystery of Life.

Just as the darkness outside you is in conflict with itself, the darkness within you is also divided. The light and fire within you represent the divine man, who rises along the path of the Word. The part that does not rise is the mortal man, who cannot share in immortality. Study the Mind and its mysteries, for in them lies the secret to eternal life."

The Dragon revealed itself once more to Hermes, and for a long time, the two stared deeply into each other's eyes. Hermes trembled under the gaze of Poimandres. At the Dragon's Word, the heavens opened, revealing countless Light Powers soaring across the Cosmos on wings of streaming fire. Hermes saw the spirits of the stars and the celestial beings that govern the universe, each glowing with the brilliance of the One Fire—the glory of the Supreme Mind. Hermes realized that this vision was shown to him only because Poimandres had spoken the Word. That Word was Reason, and by the power of Reason, the invisible had been made visible.

The Divine Mind—the Dragon—continued: "Before the visible universe existed, its mold had already been formed. This mold was called the Archetype, and it existed in the Supreme Mind long before creation began. The Supreme Mind gazed upon these Archetypes and became enchanted with Its own thoughts. Taking the Word as a powerful tool, it carved out vast spaces in the formless void, casting the spheres of creation into the Archetypal mold. At the same time, it planted the seeds of life in the newly formed bodies. When the darkness received the Word, it transformed into an ordered universe. The elements separated into layers, and from these layers, life began to emerge. The Supreme Being—the Mind, both male and female—brought forth the Word. Suspended between Light and darkness, the Word gave rise to another Mind, known as the Workman, the Master Builder, or the Maker of Things.

"This is how it was done, Hermes: As the Word moved like a breath through space, it ignited Fire through the force of its motion. Thus, the Fire is called the Son of Striving. The Workman passed like a whirlwind through the universe, making the elements vibrate and glow from the friction of its motion. From this process, the Son of Striving created the Seven Governors—the spirits of the planets— who established the boundaries of the world. These Governors control the world through Destiny, a power given to them by the Fiery Workman. Once the Second Mind (the Workman) had organized the Chaos, the Word of God emerged from the prison of material substance, leaving the elements behind without Reason. It joined itself to the Fiery Workman, and together, they settled at the center of the universe, setting the celestial powers in motion. This process will continue forever, for the beginning and the end are one and the same.

"Then the elements that lacked Reason produced creatures without it. Air gave rise to flying beings, water brought forth swimming creatures, and the earth created strange four-legged beasts, dragons, and bizarre monsters. Since Reason had risen out of material things, it could not be given to these creatures. The Father—the Supreme Mind—who is Light and Life, then created a Universal Man in Its own image. This Man was not earthly but heavenly, dwelling in the Light of God. The Supreme Mind loved the Man It had made and entrusted him with control over all creation.

"The Man, eager to create, moved into the sphere of generation and observed the works of the Second Mind, which sat upon the Ring of Fire. Seeing the achievements of the Fiery Workman, the Man desired to create as well, and the Father granted him permission. The Seven Governors, each sharing their power with him, rejoiced and gave him part of their nature.

"The Man, curious to understand the mysteries beyond the spheres, looked through the Seven Harmonies and broke through the strength of the circles. He revealed himself to Nature stretched out below. Gazing into the depths, the Man saw his own reflection upon the earth and in the waters. He smiled, enchanted by his reflection, and longed to descend into it. As soon as he desired this, the intelligent part of him united with the unreasoning image.

"Nature, seeing the Man's descent, embraced him, and the two became intertwined. This is why earthly man is a mixture of both worlds. Within him is the immortal, beautiful Sky Man, but on the outside, he is clothed in mortal Nature, which is destined to perish. Suffering arises because the Immortal Man fell in love with his shadow, giving up true Reality to dwell in the darkness of illusion. Though he possesses the power of the Seven Governors, along with Life, Light, and the Word, he is also subject to Fate and Destiny, ruled by the Rings of the Governors."

It is said that the Immortal Man is both male and female, always awake and watchful. He never slumbers or sleeps and is governed by a Father who is also both male and female, and equally watchful. This is a secret that remains hidden to this day. When Nature joined with the Sky Man, she gave birth to seven beings, each male and female, upright in form, and reflecting the qualities of the Seven Governors. These, O Hermes, are the seven races, species, and wheels of creation.

The seven beings came into existence in this way: Earth acted as the female element, while water was the male element. Fire and aether provided their spirits, and Nature formed bodies that took human shapes. The Great Dragon gave them Life and Light. From Life, they gained their Soul, and from Light, they received their Mind. These beings, containing both mortality and immortality, lived in this state for a time. They reproduced on their own, for each was both male and female. But after a certain period, God's will untied the knot of Destiny, and all things were set free.

At that time, all creatures, including man, who had been both male and female, were separated. The males were divided from the females according to the law of Reason. Then God spoke to the Holy Word within all souls, saying, "Increase and multiply, all of you, my creatures and creations. Let those with Mind know they are immortal and understand that death comes from loving the body too much. Let them learn all things, for those who know themselves will enter the realm of Good."

With the help of the Seven Governors and Harmony, God brought the sexes together, and from their union, new generations were born. Everything multiplied according to its kind. Those who mistakenly love their body remain trapped in darkness, suffering from the experience of death. But those who realize the body is only a temporary home for the soul rise to immortality.

Hermes then asked why ignorance alone should cause men to lose immortality. The Great Dragon replied, "For those who do not understand, the body is all they know. They believe in death because they worship the material world, which is both the cause and reality of death."

Hermes asked how the wise and righteous find their way to God. Poimandres answered, "What the Word of God has said, I also say: 'Since the Father of all things is made of Life and Light, and man is made from the same, whoever understands the nature of Life and Light will enter the eternal Life and Light.'"

Hermes then asked how the wise could attain eternal Life. Poimandres replied, "Let those with Mind reflect, examine themselves, and use their Mind's power to separate what is real from what is not. They must devote themselves to Truth and Reality."

Hermes asked, "Don't all people have Minds?" The Great Dragon responded, "Be careful what you say, for I am the Mind—the Eternal Teacher. I am the Father of the Word, the Savior of all men. In the nature of the wise, the Word takes form. Through the Word, the world is saved. I, Thought (Thoth)—the Father of the Word, the Mind—come only to those who are good, pure, merciful, and live faithfully and righteously. When I come, I help them understand everything, and they worship the Universal Father.

21

Before these wise people die, they learn to turn away from their senses, knowing that the senses are enemies of the immortal soul. I will not let evil desires or emotions control the bodies of those who love me, nor will I allow wicked thoughts to enter them. I guard them, shutting out all evil, and protect them from their own lower nature. But I do not come to the wicked, the envious, or the greedy, for such people cannot grasp the mysteries of the Mind and reject me. I leave them to the demon they have created within themselves. Evil grows every day, tormenting those who indulge in it, and each wicked act adds to the suffering caused by the ones that came before it. In the end, evil destroys itself. The punishment for desire is the pain of never being satisfied."

Hermes bowed his head in gratitude to the Great Dragon, who had revealed so much to him, and asked to learn more about the ultimate fate of the human soul. Poimandres continued: "At death, the material body returns to the elements from which it came, and the divine, invisible man rises to the Eighth Sphere, the place from which he first came. Evil, however, descends to the demon's domain, while the senses, emotions, desires, and bodily passions return to the Seven Governors, who give life to the spiritual man but bring destruction to the lower man.

"Once the lower nature returns to its animal instincts, the higher self begins its journey back to reclaim its spiritual state. It ascends through the seven Rings of the Seven Governors, returning to each the powers it once borrowed. The first Ring belongs to the Moon, to which it returns the ability to wax and wane. The second Ring is ruled by Mercury, where it returns cunning, deceit, and cleverness. The third Ring belongs to Venus, receiving back lust and passion. The fourth Ring is the Sun's, which takes back ambition. The fifth Ring is governed by Mars, where rashness and boldness return. The sixth belongs to Jupiter, receiving greed and the desire for wealth. Finally, the seventh Ring is Saturn's, standing at the edge of Chaos, where falsehood and evil schemes are returned.

"When the soul has shed all it carried from the Seven Rings, it reaches the Eighth Sphere, the realm of the fixed stars. There, free from illusion, the soul dwells in Light, singing praises to the Father in a voice understood only by the pure in spirit. Know this, Hermes: the Eighth Sphere holds a great mystery, for the Milky Way is where souls are born. From it, they descend into the Rings, and to it, they return after passing through the wheels of Saturn. However, not all souls can climb the ladder of the seven Rings. Some become lost in darkness below, swept away into eternity by the illusions of the senses and the material world.

"The path to immortality is difficult, and only a few find it. The rest wait for the Great Day when the wheels of the universe will stop, and the immortal sparks will escape from the prison of matter. But those who wait are unfortunate, for they will return to the Milky Way, unaware and unknowing, to begin the cycle again. Those who follow the light of the mystery I have revealed to you, Hermes, will return to the Father in the White Light. There, they will give themselves to the Light and become one with it, transformed into Powers within God. This is the Way of Good, revealed only to the wise.

"Blessed are you, O Son of Light, for I, Poimandres, the Light of the World, have shown myself to you. Now, I command you to go forth and guide those lost in darkness, so that the spirit of

My Mind—the Universal Mind—within them may awaken and be saved through My Mind within you. Establish My Mysteries, and they will remain on earth as long as the Mind endures, for the Mind of the Mysteries can never fail."

With these final words, Poimandres, radiant with celestial light, vanished, merging with the powers of the heavens. Lifting his eyes to the sky, Hermes blessed the Father of All Things and dedicated his life to the service of the Great Light.

Hermes preached: "O people of the earth, born of the elements yet carrying the spirit of the Divine Man within you, rise from your slumber of ignorance! Be alert and thoughtful. Know that your true home is not on earth but in the Light. Why have you chosen death when you have the power to share in immortality? Repent, change your ways, and turn away from darkness. Leave corruption behind and prepare to ascend through the Seven Rings to unite your soul with the eternal Light."

Some mocked him, refusing his teachings, and condemned themselves to the Second Death, from which there is no return. But others fell at Hermes' feet, begging him to show them the Way of Life. He gently lifted them, seeking no praise for himself, and with his staff in hand, he set out to teach and guide humanity, showing them the path to salvation.

Among the people, Hermes planted the seeds of wisdom and watered them with the Immortal Waters. As his life drew to a close and the light of the earthly world began to fade, Hermes instructed his disciples to guard his teachings faithfully through all ages. He committed the *Vision of Poimandres* to writing so that all who seek immortality could find the way within its pages.

In concluding his account of the Vision, Hermes wrote: "The sleep of the body allows the Mind to stay awake, and when I close my eyes, I can see the true Light. In my silence, life and hope begin to grow, filling it with goodness. My words are the blossoms that grow from the tree of my soul. This is the honest record of what I received from my true Mind—Poimandres, the Great Dragon, Lord of the Word—through whom God filled me with Truth. From that moment on, my Mind has remained with me, and within my soul, it gave birth to the Word. The Word is Reason, and through Reason, I have been saved. For this, I give all my praise and thanks to God, the Father—Life, Light, and Eternal Goodness—with all my soul and strength.

"Holy is God, the Father of all, who existed before the First Beginning. Holy is God, whose will is fulfilled by the Powers born from Himself. Holy is God, who has chosen to be known and is known only by those to whom He reveals Himself. Holy are You, who have established all things through Your Word, Reason. Holy are You, whose image is reflected in all of Nature. Holy are You, whom the lower nature cannot shape. Holy are You, who are stronger than all other powers. Holy are You, who surpass all greatness. Holy are You, who are beyond all praise.

"Accept these offerings of Reason from a pure soul and a heart lifted up toward You. O Unspeakable One, beyond words, You are to be praised through silence! I ask You to look upon me with mercy, that I may not stray from the knowledge of You and that I may help enlighten those who are lost in ignorance—my brothers, Your children.

"I believe in You and bear witness to You, and I leave in peace, trusting in Your Light and Life. Blessed are You, O Father! May the man You created be sanctified with You, just as You gave him the power to sanctify others through Your Word and Truth."

The Vision of Hermes, like many Hermetic writings, is an allegory that contains deep philosophical and spiritual truths. Its hidden meanings can only be fully understood by those who have been "raised" into the presence of the True Mind.

## The Initiation of the Pyramid

The Great Pyramid of Giza stands as one of the most remarkable wonders of ancient times, unmatched by the works of later architects and builders. It silently bears witness to a lost civilization that fulfilled its purpose and faded into history. Its grandeur is awe-inspiring, simple yet divine, and it seems like a message carved in stone. Its enormous size makes human efforts seem small, and it serves as a symbol of eternity, standing firm against the ever-shifting sands of time. But who were the enlightened mathematicians who designed it? Who were the master builders and craftsmen who made sure every stone was perfectly placed?

The earliest and most famous account of the pyramid's construction comes from the well-known historian Herodotus. He wrote: "The pyramid was built in stages, like steps or battlements. After placing the stones for the base, workers used machines made of short wooden planks to raise the stones to each new level. The first machine lifted the stones from the ground to the first step. Another machine took the stones from there to the second step, and so on. Either they had as many machines as there were steps, or they moved one machine from tier to tier as needed. Both versions have been told, so I mention them both. The upper part of the pyramid was completed first, followed by the middle section, and finally the lowest part near the ground. Egyptian characters are inscribed on the pyramid, recording the amount of radishes, onions, and garlic consumed by the laborers during construction. I remember the interpreter telling me that the food cost 1,600 talents of silver. If this is true, imagine the enormous amount spent on tools, clothing, and food for the workers during the ten years it took to complete the work, not counting the time needed to quarry the stones and prepare the underground chambers."

While Herodotus' story is vivid, it seems likely that he created this tale to hide the true origin and purpose of the pyramid. This is one of several cases in his writings that suggest he was initiated into ancient secret knowledge and was sworn to keep it hidden. The widely accepted theory that the Great Pyramid was built as a tomb for Pharaoh Cheops is unproven. In fact, Manetho, Eratosthenes, and Diodorus Siculus all offer different accounts of who built the pyramid, with none agreeing with Herodotus—or with each other. According to the rules of pyramid construction known as the Lepsius Law, the burial chamber should have been completed at the same time as the monument, or even earlier, but in this case, it wasn't.

There is no clear evidence that the Egyptians built the Great Pyramid. Unlike other royal tombs, which are decorated with intricate carvings, inscriptions, and images, the pyramid lacks these typical elements of Egyptian art and architecture. No cartouches, paintings, or symbols of Egyptian royalty are present, except for a few simple markings in construction chambers. These markings, discovered by Howard Vyse, appear to have been made before the stones were placed since they are sometimes upside down or distorted from the fitting process. Egyptologists have tried to identify these markings as the name of Cheops, but it is hard to believe that a ruler would allow his royal name to be treated with such carelessness.

Experts are still unsure of the true meaning of these markings. Any claim that the pyramid was built during the fourth dynasty is challenged by the sea shells found at its base, which Mr. Gab suggests as evidence that the structure predates the Great Flood— a theory also supported by ancient Arabian traditions. One Arab historian claimed the pyramid was built by Egyptian sages to protect against the Flood, while another said it was the treasure house of Sheddad Ben Ad, a powerful king from before the flood. A panel of hieroglyphs above the entrance might seem like a clue to the pyramid's origin, but it was actually carved in 1843 by Dr. Lepsius as a tribute to the King of Prussia.

Caliph al-Mamoun, a distinguished descendant of the Prophet, was inspired by stories of vast treasures hidden within the Great Pyramid. In 820 A.D., he traveled from Baghdad to Cairo with a large group of workers, determined to open the ancient monument. When the Caliph first stood at the base of the "Rock of Ages" and looked up at its smooth, gleaming surface, he must have felt overwhelmed with emotion. At that time, the pyramid's original casing stones were likely still intact because he could not find any sign of an entrance—just four perfectly smooth walls in every direction. Relying on vague rumors, he ordered his men to begin digging on the north side of the pyramid, instructing them to keep cutting into the stone until they uncovered something. For the workers, armed with only simple tools and vinegar to soften the limestone, digging through a hundred feet of solid rock was an exhausting and nearly impossible task. Many times, they were ready to abandon the project, but the Caliph's command was law, and the hope of finding treasure kept them going.

Just when the workers were about to give up entirely, fate intervened. They heard the sound of a large stone falling within the wall they had been chiseling. Encouraged by the noise, they pushed forward with new energy and eventually broke through into a sloping passage that led deep into the pyramid's underground chambers. They found a massive stone barrier blocking their path, but they managed to carve their way around it. Afterward, they removed several granite blocks that kept sliding down the passage from the Queen's Chamber above. Finally, the last of the blocks stopped falling, and the way was clear for the Caliph's followers to explore.

However, there were no treasures to be found. From chamber to chamber, the workers searched frantically, but there was nothing of value anywhere. The frustration among the workers grew so intense that Caliph al-Mamoun, knowing that rebellion was near, decided to take action. He secretly sent for funds from Baghdad and had the money buried near the pyramid's entrance. The next day, he ordered the workers to dig in that spot, and their joy was overwhelming when they uncovered the hidden treasure. The workers were so impressed by what they believed to be the foresight of an ancient king, who, in their minds, had calculated their wages long ago and buried the exact amount for them to find.

Satisfied with this solution, the Caliph returned to the city of his ancestors, leaving the Great Pyramid to face the passage of time. In the ninth century, the pyramid's smooth, polished surfaces reflected the sun's rays so brilliantly that each side of the structure appeared as a glowing triangle of light. Over the years, however, nearly all the original casing stones were removed, and today, only two remain in place. Investigations later found that many of these stones had been recut and repurposed to decorate the walls of mosques and palaces throughout Cairo and the surrounding areas.

• • •

# Pyramid Problems

C. Piazzi Smyth asks, "Was the Great Pyramid built before hieroglyphics were invented and before the Egyptian religion was established?" It is possible that time will reveal the upper chambers of the Pyramid as a sealed mystery even before the rise of the Egyptian empire. However, markings in the underground chamber suggest that the Romans later gained access. Based on secret Egyptian teachings, W. W. Harmon calculated that the Pyramid's first ceremonial took place 68,890 years ago, at the moment when the star Vega first cast its light down the descending passage into the pit. He estimates that the actual construction of the Pyramid took place over ten to fifteen years just before this event.

These dates may seem ridiculous to modern Egyptologists, but they are based on a detailed study of the astronomical principles incorporated into the Pyramid by its builders. If the outer casing stones were still intact in the ninth century, the erosion marks on the exterior are unlikely to have been caused by water. The theory that salt deposits inside the Pyramid are evidence of submersion is also questionable, as the type of stone used naturally releases salt over time. Although the Pyramid may have been partially submerged at some point, the evidence for this is not conclusive.

The Great Pyramid was built entirely from limestone and granite, with the two types of rock arranged in a meaningful way. The stones were cut with extreme precision, and the cement used between them is now as hard as the stones themselves. The limestone blocks were likely cut with bronze saws tipped with diamonds or other precious stones. Stone chips left from construction were piled against the north side of the plateau to help support the structure's immense weight. The Pyramid was built with perfect alignment and, astonishingly, "squares the circle." This means that if you drop a vertical line from the tip of the Pyramid to its base, that line acts as the radius of an imaginary circle. The circumference of that circle matches the total length of the four base sides of the Pyramid.

If the passageways to the King's and Queen's Chambers were sealed thousands of years before the Christian era, later initiates must have used hidden underground galleries for their rituals. Without such galleries, it would have been impossible to enter or exit the Pyramid, as the only surface entrance was sealed with casing stones. If not blocked by the Sphinx or concealed within it, the hidden entrance could be located in one of the nearby temples or on the slopes of the limestone plateau.

A notable feature of the Pyramid is the granite plugs that block the passage leading to the Queen's Chamber. Caliph al-Mamoun had to smash through these plugs to reach the upper chambers. According to Smyth, the position of the stones shows that they were set in place from above, suggesting that many workers had to leave the upper chambers after placing them. Smyth believes these workers escaped by descending through a well, dropping a ramp stone into place behind them. He also suggests that robbers might have later used this well to reach the upper chambers. The robbers broke through the ramp stone, leaving a jagged hole, as it had been set in plaster.

However, the architect Mr. Dupré offers a different theory. He argues that the well itself was made by robbers and was the first successful attempt to reach the upper chambers from the underground chamber, which was the only open area of the Pyramid at the time. Dupré points out that the well is rough and irregular, unlike the precise design of the rest of the Pyramid. The well's size also makes it unlikely that it was dug downward; it must have been carved from below, with the nearby grotto providing ventilation for the thieves. It seems unlikely that the Pyramid's builders would have left a broken ramp stone and a gaping hole in their otherwise perfect gallery. If the well is indeed a robbers' tunnel, this could explain why the Pyramid was empty when Caliph al-Mamoun entered and why the coffer lid was missing. A thorough inspection of the unfinished underground chamber—possibly the robbers' base of operations—might reveal traces of their presence or show where they stored the rubble from their digging. It remains unclear how the robbers entered the underground chamber, but it seems unlikely that they used the descending passage.

One intriguing feature in the Queen's Chamber is a niche in the north wall. Muslim guides often describe it as a shrine, but the niche's shape, with its walls sloping inward like those in the Grand Gallery, suggests it may have been intended as a passage. Attempts to explore the niche have been unsuccessful, but Dupré believes it may hide a secret entrance. If the well did not exist at the time, the workers may have exited the Pyramid through this hidden passage after placing the granite plugs in the ascending gallery.

Some Biblical scholars have offered remarkable interpretations of the Great Pyramid. They have claimed it to be Joseph's granary, even though its storage capacity is far too small to support that idea. Others have suggested it was meant to serve as the tomb for the Pharaoh from the Exodus, though his body was never recovered from the Red Sea and, therefore, couldn't have been buried there. Some even believe the pyramid stands as a lasting confirmation of the accuracy of the prophecies found in the Authorized Version of the Bible.

• • •

# The Sphinx

Ignatius Donnelly suggests that the Great Pyramid follows a design from before the Great Flood, a style found in many ancient cultures around the world. In contrast, the Sphinx (Hu) is distinctly Egyptian. According to the inscription between its paws, the Sphinx is an image of the Sun God, Harmachis, carved in the likeness of the Pharaoh who ruled at the time. The Sphinx was later restored by Thutmose IV, inspired by a dream in which the god complained that the sand surrounding him caused him great discomfort. Excavators even found a broken beard of the Sphinx buried between its paws. The steps, altar, and temple between the paws were added much later, likely by the Romans, who frequently rebuilt Egyptian monuments.

The shallow indentation on the Sphinx's head, once thought to conceal a hidden passage leading to the Great Pyramid, was actually intended to support a now-missing headdress. Explorers have driven metal rods into the body of the Sphinx in an unsuccessful attempt to locate hidden chambers or tunnels. Most of the Sphinx was carved from a single stone, with only the front paws constructed from smaller stones. Measuring around 200 feet in length, 70 feet in height, and 38 feet across the shoulders, the Sphinx was carved either from native rock or from stone transported from distant quarries. Some once believed that both the Pyramid and the Sphinx were made from artificial stone formed on-site, but this idea was abandoned after studies showed that the limestone contains the remains of small sea creatures called mummulites.

The idea that the Sphinx served as the entrance to the Great Pyramid is a popular belief that has persisted, though without any real proof. P. Christian, drawing from the writings of Iamblichus, describes the theory this way: "The Sphinx of Giza marked the entrance to underground chambers where initiates faced trials. The entrance, now blocked by sand and debris, lay between the Sphinx's front legs. In ancient times, a bronze door guarded this entrance, which could only be opened by the Magi through a secret mechanism. Public respect and religious fear kept the entrance safe from intrusion. Inside the Sphinx, tunnels led to the underground chambers of the Great Pyramid, forming a maze so complex that anyone entering without a guide would inevitably circle back to where they began."

However, there is no sign of the bronze door Christian mentions, nor any evidence it ever existed. Over the centuries, the Sphinx has undergone many changes, and it is possible that any original entrance was sealed. Many believe that underground chambers still exist beneath the Great Pyramid. Robert Ballard writes, "Just as the priests of the Pyramids of Lake Moeris lived in vast underground quarters, it seems likely that the priests of Giza had similar residences. In fact, the limestone used to build the pyramids might have been excavated from these underground caverns. I am convinced that exploring beneath the Pyramid will reveal important clues about its purpose. A diamond drill capable of reaching a few hundred feet would be needed to investigate both the solidity of the Pyramid and any hidden spaces beneath it."

Ballard's theory raises an important architectural question. The Pyramid's builders were too skilled to place over five million tons of stone on anything but a solid foundation. If there are underground chambers, they must be small and well-supported, much like the chambers inside the Pyramid, which occupy only a tiny fraction of its total volume.

The Sphinx was likely created for symbolic purposes under the direction of the priesthood. Some theories suggest that the Sphinx once had a uraeus, or serpent symbol, on its forehead that served as the pointer of a giant sundial. Others believe both the Pyramid and the Sphinx were used to track time, the seasons, and the precession of the equinoxes. If the Sphinx was built to block access to a hidden passage leading to an underground temple within the Pyramid, its symbolic meaning would be fitting. However, compared to the majesty and scale of the Pyramid, the Sphinx seems relatively insignificant.

Today, the face of the Sphinx, which still shows traces of the red paint it was originally covered with, is heavily damaged. Its nose was broken off by a devout Muslim who feared it might lead people toward idol worship. The repairs now required to keep the head from collapsing suggest that the Sphinx could not have survived the same vast stretches of time as the Pyramid.

To the Egyptians, the Sphinx symbolized both strength and intelligence. Its androgynous form reflected the belief that initiates and gods contained both masculine and feminine energies. Gerald Massey explains, "This is the secret of the Sphinx. The Egyptian sphinx is male in the front and female in the back. The image of Sut-Typhon follows the same pattern, with horns and a tail— male at the front and female at the back. Pharaohs, too, wore the tail of a lioness or cow behind them, representing the union of both sexes within themselves. Like the gods, they embodied the complete dual nature of existence."

Despite its symbolic importance, many researchers have dismissed the Sphinx, choosing instead to focus on the greater mystery of the Pyramid.

• • •

# The Pyramid Mysteries

The word "pyramid" is often thought to come from the Greek word *pyr,* meaning fire, symbolizing the divine flame that gives life to all beings. John Taylor believed the word referred to a "measure of wheat," while C. Piazzi Smyth suggested it meant "a division into ten" in Coptic. Ancient initiates saw the pyramid shape as a perfect symbol for both their hidden teachings and the institutions created to spread this wisdom. Pyramids and mounds were thought to represent the Holy Mountain, a sacred place believed to stand at the center of the earth. John P. Lundy compared the Great Pyramid to Mount Olympus, saying its underground passages were like the winding paths of Hades.

The square base of the Pyramid symbolizes that the foundation of wisdom rests on nature's unchanging laws. Albert Pike wrote that the Gnostics built their knowledge on a square whose corners represented Silence, Profundity, Intelligence, and Truth. The four sides of the Great Pyramid align with the cardinal directions: north and south, which represent cold and heat, and east and west, which stand for light and darkness. The base also represents the four material elements from which the physical body is formed. Rising from each side is a triangle, symbolizing the divine being that dwells within all material forms. If each base line is treated as a square from which spiritual power rises, the total of the lines on the four sides (12) and the squares of the base (16) is 28, a sacred number. Adding the three sets of seven that represent the sun (21) gives 49, the square of seven, which symbolizes the universe.

The twelve zodiac signs are represented by the twelve edges of the Pyramid's four triangular faces. Within each face is one of the four creatures from the vision of Ezekiel, turning the entire structure into a representation of the Cherubim. The three main chambers of the Pyramid correspond to the heart, the brain, and the reproductive system—key spiritual centers in human beings. The Pyramid's triangular shape also mirrors the posture used in ancient meditation practices. According to the Mysteries, divine energy descended from the gods onto the Pyramid's tip, which was compared to the roots of an inverted tree, with branches spreading downward along the Pyramid's sides, radiating wisdom throughout the world.

No one knows the exact size of the Pyramid's capstone, and although many believe it once existed, it is now missing. It's common for builders of sacred structures to leave them unfinished, as a reminder that only God is complete. If the capstone did exist, it would have been a miniature pyramid, with a smaller version of itself on top, continuing infinitely. This capstone represents the entire structure in miniature. Similarly, the Pyramid can be seen as a symbol of the universe, with the capstone representing humanity. Within each person, the mind is the capstone of the body, the spirit is the capstone of the mind, and God is the final capstone of the spirit. Just as a rough stone is shaped into a perfect capstone, the Mysteries transform a person into the living apex through which divine energy flows into the world below.

W. Marsham Adams called the Great Pyramid the "House of the Hidden Places" because it symbolized the secret wisdom that predated Egyptian civilization. The Egyptians linked the Pyramid to Hermes, the god of wisdom and knowledge, also associated with the planet Mercury. Connecting Hermes with the Pyramid emphasizes that the structure was a temple dedicated to the Invisible and Supreme Deity. It was not built as a tomb, observatory, or lighthouse, but as the first temple of the Mysteries—a place that guarded the truths at the heart of all knowledge and science. The Pyramid perfectly represents the microcosm (the small world) and the macrocosm (the larger universe). According to secret teachings, it was also considered the tomb of Osiris, the black god of the Nile, who symbolizes a form of solar energy. His tomb represents the universe, where Osiris is both buried and crucified on the cross of material existence.

Through the hidden passages and chambers of the Great Pyramid, the enlightened ones of ancient times made their journey. They entered as ordinary men and emerged as gods. The Pyramid was known as the "womb of the Mysteries," a place of "second birth," where wisdom lived just as God lives within the hearts of people. Deep within its recesses dwelled a mysterious figure called "The Initiator" or "The Illustrious One." This being, dressed in blue and gold and holding the sevenfold key of Eternity, was the lion-faced teacher, the Holy One, and the Master of Masters. He never left the House of Wisdom, and no one saw him unless they had first gone through the trials of preparation and purification. It was in these sacred chambers that Plato, the philosopher with the broad brow, encountered ancient wisdom personified in the Master of the Hidden House.

Who was this Master who lived within the Pyramid, whose many chambers symbolized the worlds of the universe? Only those who had been "born again" could see him. He alone knew the deepest secrets of the Pyramid, but now he has left, and the sacred halls are empty. No longer do hymns of praise echo through the corridors. No one now passes through the elements or walks among the seven stars. The "Word of Life" is no longer given to the worthy by the lips of the Eternal One. All that remains visible to the world is an empty shell—an outer symbol of an inner truth—and people call this House of God a tomb.

The Master of the Secret House, the Sage Illuminator, revealed the techniques of the Mysteries to new initiates. He showed them how to recognize their guardian spirit and taught them how to free their spiritual essence from the physical body. At the height of their transformation, he shared the Divine Name—the secret and unspoken title of the Supreme Deity. With this knowledge, the initiate became like a pyramid within his soul, where others could find their own spiritual awakening.

In the King's Chamber, the initiate underwent the ritual of the "second death." There, after being symbolically crucified upon the cross of the solstices and equinoxes, he was placed in the great stone coffer. The King's Chamber had a strange and deathly cold that seemed to reach into the bones. This sacred space acted as a gateway between the physical world and the higher realms of Nature. While the initiate's body rested in the coffer, his soul, like a human-headed hawk, soared through the celestial realms. In these realms, he saw the truth of eternal Life, Light, and Truth and understood that Death, Darkness, and Sin were mere illusions. In this way, the Great Pyramid served as a gateway through which the ancient priests allowed a few to reach spiritual completion.

If someone strikes the coffer in the King's Chamber, the sound it makes does not match any known musical scale. This unique tone may have been part of what made the King's Chamber the ideal place to perform the highest rites of the Mysteries.

Modern science and theology know little about these ancient rituals. Scholars look at the Great Pyramid and wonder what motivated such immense labor. But if they paused to reflect, they might realize that only one thing could inspire such effort: the soul's deep desire to understand, to know the truth, and to exchange mortal limitation for divine knowledge. People today say the Great Pyramid is the most perfect building ever made, the origin of weights and measures, the first Noah's Ark, and the source of alphabets, languages, and even scales for measuring temperature and humidity. Few realize, however, that it is also a gateway to the Eternal.

Though the modern world may hold countless secrets, the ancient world held one—and that one was greater than all others. The many secrets of today lead to death, sorrow, selfishness, greed, and destruction, but the one secret of the past brings life, light, and truth. A time will come when the ancient wisdom will once again guide humanity's religious and philosophical search. The collapse of rigid dogmas is near. The "Tower of Babel," with its confusion of languages, was built from bricks of mud held together by slime. But from the ashes of dead creeds, the ancient Mysteries will rise like a phoenix. No other institution has ever fulfilled humanity's spiritual needs as completely as the Mysteries. Since their destruction, no religious system has emerged that someone like Plato could fully embrace. The development of the human spirit is as precise a science as astronomy, medicine, or law. Religion was created for this very purpose, and from it arose philosophy, science, and logic as tools to achieve this divine goal.

The Dying God will rise again! The hidden chamber in the House of Secrets will be rediscovered. The Pyramid will once more stand as a symbol of strength, renewal, aspiration, resurrection, and transformation. As one civilization after another is buried beneath the sands of time, the Pyramid will remain as a visible reminder of the eternal connection between divine wisdom and the world. One day, the ancient hymns of enlightenment will again echo through its halls. The Master of the Hidden House will wait in the Silent Place for those who, leaving behind the false ideas of dogma, seek only Truth and will not settle for anything less than the real thing.

## Isis, the Virgin of the World

The study of Hermetic symbolism often begins with the figure of the Saitic Isis, a version of the goddess from the city of Sais. Her temple bore the famous inscription: "I, Isis, am all that has been, that is, or shall be; no mortal man has ever lifted my veil." According to Plutarch, some ancient authors believed Isis was the daughter of Hermes, while others thought she was the child of Prometheus. Both were known for their divine wisdom, though her connection to them may be symbolic rather than literal. Plutarch also interpreted the name Isis to mean wisdom. In *Anacalypsis*,

Godfrey Higgins traced her name to the Hebrew word *Iso* and the Greek word *zoo*, meaning "to save." Other scholars, like Richard Payne Knight, suggested her name had Northern origins, possibly from Scandinavian or Gothic languages, where it is pronounced *Isa*, meaning "ice" or "frozen water."

This goddess, known by many names, represented fertility across various ancient religions. She was sometimes called the "goddess with ten thousand names" and, over time, was transformed in Christian tradition into the Virgin Mary. Although Isis was believed to have given birth to all living things—especially the sun—legend says she remained a virgin.

In *The Golden Ass*, Apuleius includes a description of Isis where she declares her divine attributes: "I am Nature, the mother of all things, ruler of the elements, first among the gods, queen of the dead, and leader of the celestial beings. The entire world honors me with different names and rituals. The Phrygians call me Pessinuntica, the Mother of the Gods. The Athenians name me Cecropian Minerva, the Cypriots call me Paphian Venus, and the Cretans know me as Diana. The Sicilians worship me as Proserpine, and the Eleusinians as Ceres. Others call me Juno, Bellona, Hecate, or Rhamnusia. In Ethiopia, Egypt, and among the Arii, where the sun's light is strong, I am known by my true name: Queen Isis."

Some historians, like Le Plongeon, believe that the story of Isis has historical roots among the Mayans of Central America, where she was known as Queen Moo, and her brother-husband Osiris was represented as Prince Coh. According to this theory, Queen Moo fled to Egypt after Prince Coh's death, where she was accepted as queen and given the name Isis. However, the global presence of Isis in so many myths suggests that she was likely more of a symbolic figure than a real person.

Sextus Empiricus claims that the Trojan War was fought over a statue of the moon goddess, not for the mortal Helen, as commonly believed. Some authors have even tried to connect figures like Isis, Osiris, Typhon, and Thoth to the descendants of Noah's son, Ham. But since the story of Noah is more of a cosmic allegory about the renewal of life, it is unlikely that these Egyptian deities were ever real historical figures.

According to Robert Fludd, the sun embodies life, light, and heat—qualities that energize the three realms of existence: the spiritual, intellectual, and physical worlds. This is summarized by the phrase, "From one light, three lights," which reflects the sun's role in bringing life and vitality to the earth. Osiris, therefore, symbolizes the life-giving power of the sun, though not the sun itself. His symbol was an open eye, representing the "Great Eye" of the universe—the sun—while Isis symbolized the receptive force of Nature.

Modern science has shown that everything, from stars to atoms, follows a pattern of positive centers surrounded by negative bodies that depend on the central life force. This allegory is echoed in the story of Solomon and his many wives, where Solomon represents the sun, and his wives are the planets and moons orbiting it. In *The Song of Solomon*, the dark maid of Jerusalem symbolizes Isis, representing the nurturing force of Nature that gives life after being energized by the sun.

The ancient year consisted of 360 days, with five extra days set aside as the birthdays of five gods and goddesses—Osiris being born on the first day, and Isis on the fourth. Typhon, the spirit of destruction, was born on the third day and is often represented as a crocodile or a mixture of crocodile and pig. Isis stood for wisdom, while Typhon symbolized arrogance and pride—traits that block understanding and truth.

The story continues with Osiris, symbolizing the sun, bringing knowledge to Egypt and traveling to other lands to spread enlightenment. Meanwhile, his brother Typhon plotted against him. Like the Norse trickster Loki, Typhon gathered conspirators and devised a plan to trap Osiris. He commissioned a beautifully decorated chest, perfectly sized to fit Osiris's body. During a banquet, Typhon invited the gods to lie inside the chest, promising to give it to whoever fit inside perfectly. When Osiris tried it, Typhon sealed the chest with molten lead and cast it into the Nile, where it floated out to sea. According to Plutarch, this event occurred on the seventeenth day of the month Athyr, when the sun was in Scorpio—a symbol of betrayal. This story also parallels the moment when Noah entered the ark to escape the flood.

Plutarch also says that the Pans and Satyrs, which are nature spirits and elementals, were the first to find out that Osiris had been killed. As soon as they discovered this, they raised an alarm, and from this event, we get the word "panic," which means fear or amazement felt by many people. Isis found out about her husband's death from some children who saw the killers running off with the box that held his body. She immediately dressed in mourning clothes and began her search for him.

47

Eventually, Isis discovered that the chest had floated to the shores of Byblos. There, it got stuck in the branches of a tree that quickly grew around it in a miraculous way. The king of that land was so amazed by the tree that he ordered it to be cut down and turned into a pillar to hold up the roof of his palace. When Isis arrived in Byblos, she was able to get her husband's body back, but Typhon stole it again. This time, he cut Osiris's body into fourteen pieces and scattered them across the earth. In despair, Isis began gathering the parts of her husband but could only find thirteen. The missing piece, the phallus, had fallen into the Nile River and been swallowed by a fish, so Isis made a replacement out of gold.

Later, Osiris's son killed Typhon in battle. Some Egyptians believed that the souls of gods went to heaven, where they became stars. They thought the soul of Isis shined from the Dog Star, while Typhon became the constellation of the Bear. However, it is unclear if this belief was widely accepted. In Egyptian art, Isis is often shown wearing a headdress shaped like the empty throne of her dead husband, which became her symbol during certain periods. The headdresses worn by Egyptians carry deep symbolic meaning, representing the spiritual energy around divine beings, much like halos and auras in Christian art. Frank C. Higgins, a well-known Masonic expert on symbols, noted that the way some Egyptian gods and pharaohs wore their headpieces at a backward tilt mirrored the tilt of the earth's axis. The clothing, jewelry, and ornaments of ancient priests symbolized the spiritual energy radiating from the human body. Modern science is starting to rediscover some of the lost knowledge from Hermetic philosophy. One of these discoveries is the ability to measure a person's mental, spiritual, and physical state by observing the streams of barely visible electric energy that flow from the surface of their skin throughout their life. (For more details on how this energy can be seen using a scientific process, see *The Human Atmosphere* by Dr. Walter J. Kilner.)

Isis is sometimes symbolized with the head of a cow, and in some cases, the whole animal represents her. In Norse mythology, the first gods were said to be licked out of ice blocks by a mother cow named Audhumla, who symbolized natural nourishment and fertility because of her milk. Isis is also depicted as a bird in some representations. She often holds the crux ansata, a symbol of eternal life, in one hand, and a flowered scepter representing her authority in the other.

Thoth Hermes Trismegistus, known as the founder of Egyptian knowledge and one of the wisest figures in history, passed down the ancient secrets that are still preserved today through myths and legends. These stories and symbols hide instructions for spiritual, mental, moral, and physical transformation, which is often referred to as the "Mystic Chemistry of the Soul," or alchemy. These sacred truths were shared with those initiated into the Mystery Schools but kept hidden from the general public. People who couldn't understand the deeper meaning of these teachings ended up worshiping the statues and symbols that represented these hidden truths. The wisdom and secrecy of Egypt are perfectly captured in the image of the Sphinx, which has kept its secrets safe for countless generations of seekers.

The mysteries of Hermeticism contain great spiritual truths that remain hidden from most of the world because of ignorance. The keys to these ancient teachings are all symbolized by the figure of the Virgin Isis. She is depicted veiled from head to toe, revealing her wisdom only to those who have earned the right to stand in her presence. These worthy few can uncover the hidden knowledge of nature and confront the deeper reality of the divine directly.

The descriptions of the symbols associated with the Virgin Isis in this text are mainly drawn from a free translation of the fourth book of *Bibliotèque des Philosophes Hermétiques*, titled "The Hermetical Signification of the Symbols and Attributes of Isis," with extra notes added by the writer to explain and clarify the ideas. Statues of Isis were decorated with images of the sun, moon, stars, and other symbols connected to the earth, which she was believed to rule as the guardian spirit of Nature itself. Many statues of the goddess have been found with their original symbols intact, showing the respect and status she held. Ancient philosophers viewed her as a symbol of Universal Nature, the source of all creation. She was often depicted as a partly nude woman, sometimes pregnant, and sometimes covered in a flowing robe, usually in green or black. In some cases, her clothing was a mix of black, white, yellow, and red.

Apuleius described her in great detail: "Her long hair flowed down her neck in soft, loose strands, and a crown made from many flowers rested on her head. In the center of this crown was a round object that looked like a mirror, or more like a bright, glowing light, representing the moon. Vipers, coiled like plowed furrows, wound around the crown on both sides, and ears of corn extended upward. Her robe, made from the finest linen, shimmered with many colors—white like light, yellow like crocus flowers, and rosy red. However, the part of her clothing that stood out most was a black robe that glittered darkly. It draped across her right side, rose over her left shoulder, and gathered at the front, looking like the center of a shield. The ends of this robe hung in graceful folds, with delicate tassels at the edges. Stars were scattered across the embroidery, and in the middle of these stars, the full moon shone brightly, radiating light like fire. A crown made of flowers and fruits of all kinds ran along the edge of the robe, moving with each graceful motion. In one hand, she held a bronze rattle called a sistrum, which made a sharp, triple sound as it shook. In the other hand, she carried a long, narrow vessel shaped like a boat, with the head of an asp rising from the handle, its neck swollen as if ready to strike. Her immortal feet were wrapped in shoes woven from palm leaves, symbolizing victory."

The green in her robe represents the plants that cover the earth, symbolizing Nature's clothing. The black color stands for death and decay, which lead to new life. This idea reflects the saying: "Unless someone is born again, they cannot see the kingdom of God" (John 3:3). The white, yellow, and red represent the three main colors used in alchemy, following the blackness that symbolizes decay and transformation. The name "Isis" was also used for one of the secret medicines of the ancient world, which shows that this description has connections to chemistry. Her black robe symbolizes the moon's dependence on the sun, as the moon has no light of its own but reflects the sun's light, energy, and life-giving power. Isis also represents the greatest achievements of ancient wisdom—like the Philosopher's Stone, the Elixir of Life, and the Universal Medicine.

Other symbols related to Isis are just as fascinating, but it's impossible to list them all since the Egyptian Hermetists often used them interchangeably. Isis is sometimes shown wearing a hat made from cypress branches, symbolizing her mourning for her dead husband, as well as the physical death that all living things must undergo to achieve new life or rebirth. At times, her head is decorated with a crown of gold or a wreath of olive leaves, which show her power as the queen of the world and ruler of the universe. The golden crown also represents the fiery energy of the sun, which gives life to all beings by maintaining the balance of the elements. This ongoing cycle of energy is symbolized by the musical sistrum she carries, which also represents purity.

A serpent woven through the olive leaves on her head, biting its own tail, symbolizes how the energy from the sun becomes tainted by earthly corruption. This energy must undergo purification through seven stages, called "planetary circulations" or "flying eagles" in alchemical terms, to restore it to its healing power. The sun's energy is seen as a kind of medicine for human illnesses. These seven stages are symbolized in different rituals, such as the seven circuits made by Masons around their lodge, the Jewish priests' seven marches around Jericho, and the Muslim priests' seven rounds around the Kaaba in Mecca. From the crown of gold rise three horns of plenty, which represent the abundance of Nature's gifts, all coming from one source—the heavens, symbolized by the head of Isis.

In this image, ancient thinkers describe the forces that sustain the three kingdoms of nature: minerals, plants, and animals (including humans). At one ear, the moon, and at the other, the sun represent two essential forces—one active, the other receptive, like father and mother. Isis, who symbolizes Nature, uses these two celestial bodies to spread her power across the realms of animals, plants, and minerals. On her neck, there are symbols of planets and zodiac signs, showing that heavenly forces influence the growth and destiny of all living things. These forces guide everything under the moon and shape smaller worlds that reflect the larger universe.

In her right hand, Isis holds a small ship with a spinning wheel as its mast. At the top of the mast is a water jug with a snake-shaped handle, full of venom. This shows that Isis guides the fragile ship of life through the storms of time. The spinning wheel represents how she spins and cuts the thread of life. These symbols also suggest that Isis brings moisture to everything in nature, protecting life from the sun's heat by keeping things hydrated with moisture from the air. Water helps plants grow, but this life-giving moisture often carries poison caused by decay. To make this moisture pure, it must encounter Nature's invisible cleansing fire. This fire refines, perfects, and re-energizes the substance, turning it into a healing power that can renew all life.

The snake sheds its skin every year, symbolizing the renewal of the spirit after material life. The earth also renews itself every spring when the sun returns to the northern lands. In her left hand, the symbolic Virgin carries a sistrum and a square cymbal, which produces the key-note of Nature (Fa) when struck. Sometimes, she also holds an olive branch, representing the harmony she brings to nature with her renewing power. Through death and decay, she brings forth new life in endless cycles. The square shape of the cymbal, rather than the usual triangle, shows that all things are transformed according to the balance of the four elements.

Dr. Sigismund Bacstrom believed that if a doctor could balance earth, fire, air, and water, and bring them together into the Philosopher's Stone, represented by a six-pointed star or two interlocking triangles, they could heal any disease. Dr. Bacstrom also believed the universal fire or spirit of Nature was present in everything: "It does all and is all." Through attraction, repulsion, movement, heat, evaporation, drying, thickening, and fixing, this spirit shapes matter and reveals itself in creation. Anyone who understands these natural laws and uses them wisely becomes a true philosopher.

From Isis's right breast, a cluster of grapes emerges, and from her left, an ear of corn or wheat, golden in color. This shows that Nature provides food for plants, animals, and people, nourishing all life. The golden color of the wheat suggests that within sunlight or spiritual gold lies the essence of life itself. Around the upper part of her body is a belt with mysterious symbols. This belt is held together at the front by four golden plates, arranged in a square, symbolizing the four elements—earth, air, fire, and water—that create everything. Stars also appear on this belt, symbolizing the influence of both sunlight and darkness. Isis is identified with the constellation Virgo, where she is depicted with a serpent under her feet and a crown of stars on her head. In her arms, she holds a sheaf of grain and, at times, the young Sun God.

The statue of Isis was placed on a pedestal made of dark stone, decorated with the heads of rams. Beneath her feet were several poisonous snakes. This shows that Nature has the power to remove harmful substances and cleanse all impurities caused by earthly decay. The rams' heads represent that the best time for life to begin is when the sun moves through Aries. The snakes under her feet symbolize Nature's ability to preserve life and cure illness by getting rid of impurities and decay.

This idea reflects the wisdom of ancient philosophers, who expressed it with these sayings:

Nature contains Nature,

Nature delights in her own nature,

Nature surpasses Nature,

Nature can only be corrected through her own nature.

Thus, when thinking about the statue of Isis, it is important to consider the deeper meanings behind the symbols. If we do not, the Virgin's message will remain a mystery.

A golden ring on her left arm holds a cord, which extends to a deep container filled with glowing coals and incense. This shows that Isis, as a symbol of Nature, carries with her the sacred fire, which was always kept burning by temple priestesses called vestal virgins. This flame represents the pure, eternal spirit of Nature—the essence of life itself. The oil that never burns away, known as the balsam of life, is often mentioned by wise thinkers and in religious texts, symbolizing the fuel that sustains this everlasting flame.

From her right arm hangs another thread, connected to a pair of scales. This represents Nature's precision in balancing all things, as she weighs and measures them perfectly. Isis is often shown as a symbol of justice, reflecting Nature's unwavering consistency. The World Virgin is sometimes depicted standing between two tall pillars, known in Freemasonry as Jachin and Boaz. These pillars represent the idea that Nature creates by balancing opposites. Isis, as a figure of wisdom, stands between these opposites, showing that true understanding is found in balance and that truth often appears hidden between conflicting ideas.

The golden shine in her dark hair represents how her power, although connected to the moon, comes from the sun's light, giving her a reddish glow. Just as the moon reflects the sun's light, Isis is portrayed like the Virgin in Revelation, bathed in the brightness of the sun. The writer Apuleius describes a vision in which he saw the goddess Isis rising from the ocean. The ancient people understood that life began in water, and modern science agrees. In *Outline of History*, H.G. Wells explains how early life filled the oceans, but the land above the tide was barren and lifeless. Later, he writes, "Wherever the shoreline ran, there was life, and that life existed through water, in water, and with water as its essential element."

The ancients believed that the seeds of life came from warm, moist vapor. The veiled figure of Isis symbolizes this vapor, which carries the life force from the sun, shown by the child she holds in her arms. Since the sun, moon, and stars appear to sink into the sea when they set, and the water absorbs their light, people believed the sea was the source of life's seeds. These seeds were thought to be formed through the combined influence of the celestial bodies. That is why Isis is sometimes shown as being pregnant.

The statue of Isis was often shown with a large ox that was black and white. The ox symbolized either Osiris, connected to Taurus, the bull in the zodiac, or Apis, a sacred bull linked to Osiris because of its special patterns and colors. In Egyptian culture, bulls were used for hard labor, reminding people that Nature works patiently to keep all living things healthy and alive. Alongside Isis, the figure of Harpocrates, the God of Silence, is often shown with a finger held to his mouth, signaling that the secrets of the wise must be kept from those who are not ready to understand them.

The Druids of Britain and Gaul knew much about the mysteries of Isis and worshiped her through the symbol of the moon. However, Godfrey Higgins believed it was wrong to see Isis as identical to the moon itself. Instead, the moon was used to represent her because it controls water. The Druids saw the sun as the father and the moon as the mother of all creation, and through these symbols, they honored the power of Universal Nature.

Sometimes, the figure of Isis stands for mystical and magical practices such as necromancy, spell-casting, and miracle-working. One myth tells of how Isis used her magic to make Ra, the powerful God of Eternity, reveal his secret, sacred name. This name is thought to be like the Lost Word of Masonry, which gives those who know it power over unseen and higher beings. The priests of Isis mastered these hidden forces of Nature, practicing things like hypnotism and mesmerism long before the modern world understood them.

Plutarch described what it takes to follow Isis, saying: "Just as a beard or rough clothing does not make a philosopher, neither do frequent shavings or wearing linen make someone a true follower of Isis. Only the one who listens, learns the stories of these gods properly, and seeks out the hidden meaning behind them, guided by reason and wisdom, is a true servant of this goddess."

During the Middle Ages, the troubadours of Central Europe kept the legends of Isis alive in their songs. They wrote poems about the most beautiful woman in the world, though her true identity was rarely known. She was Sophia, the Virgin of Wisdom, whom philosophers throughout history have sought to understand. Isis represents the mystery of motherhood, which ancient people saw as the greatest example of Nature's wisdom and proof of divine power. To those seeking truth today, Isis symbolizes the Great Unknown, and only those who uncover her mysteries can truly understand life, death, birth, and renewal.

• • •

# Mummification of The Egyptian Dead

Servius, commenting on Virgil's *Æneid*, notes that "the wise Egyptians carefully embalmed their bodies and placed them in catacombs so that the soul would stay connected to the body for a long time, preventing it from wandering off too soon. On the other hand, the Romans, with the opposite goal, burned the bodies of their dead on funeral pyres, hoping the soul would quickly return to the original, universal element." (From Prichard's *An Analysis of the Egyptian Mythology*.)

There are no complete records revealing the Egyptians' secret beliefs about how the soul, or consciousness, was connected to the body. However, it seems likely that Pythagoras, who was initiated into the Egyptian temples, shared parts of these teachings when he introduced the idea of metempsychosis, or the soul's migration from one body to another. The common idea that Egyptians mummified their dead to preserve the body for a future physical resurrection does not align with modern understanding of their philosophy about death. In the fourth book of *On Abstinence from Animal Food*, Porphyry explains that the Egyptians purified the dead by removing the internal organs and placing them in a separate chest. He also shares a prayer, translated from Egyptian by Euphantus, which says:

"O sovereign Sun, and all you Gods who give life to humans, receive me and bring me to the eternal Gods to dwell with them. For I have faithfully honored the gods my parents taught me to worship during my life. I also showed respect for those who gave me life. As for other people, I have neither killed anyone nor cheated anyone of anything entrusted to me. I have committed no serious wrong. If I have done anything wrong by eating or drinking what was forbidden, the fault lies not with me but with these." (Here, the speaker points to the chest containing the organs.)

The Egyptians believed that removing the organs, which were seen as the source of cravings, purified the body by freeing it from their harmful influence.

Early Christians took their scriptures so literally that they preserved bodies by soaking them in salt water, believing this would ensure the spirit could return to a whole and intact body on the day of resurrection. They avoided embalming or removing internal organs, fearing that doing so would stop the soul from returning to the body. Instead, they buried their dead without using the Egyptians' complex mummification practices.

In *Egyptian Magic*, S.S.D.D. offers an interesting theory about the hidden purpose behind mummification. He writes, "It seems likely that only those who had reached a certain level of initiation were mummified. To the Egyptians, mummification prevented reincarnation, which was only required for souls that had failed the initiation tests. Those with the strength and wisdom to enter the Secret Adytum did not need to reincarnate. Their bodies were preserved as a kind of talisman or material anchor for the soul to return to earth when needed."

In its early stages, mummification was reserved for Pharaohs and members of the royal family, who were believed to share some of the qualities of Osiris, the divine king of the underworld, who was also mummified.

## The Sun, A Universal Deity

Worship of the sun was one of the earliest and most natural ways people expressed their faith. Many modern religious beliefs are just more complicated versions of this simple, original idea. Early humans, recognizing the life-giving power of the sun, honored it as a representative of the Supreme Being. Albert Pike explains the origin of sun worship in *Morals and Dogma* by saying: "To them [early people], he [the sun] was the inner fire within all things, the fire of Nature. As the source of life, warmth, and energy, the sun was seen as the power behind all creation. Without him, there could be no movement, no life, and no shape to anything. He seemed vast, eternal, and always present. People felt a deep need for his light and creative force, and nothing frightened them more than his absence. His kindness and life-giving energy made him a symbol of Good. The BRAHMA of the Hindus, MITHRAS of the Persians, and ATHOM, AMUN, PHTHA, and OSIRIS of the Egyptians, along with the BEL of the Chaldeans, the ADONAI of the Phoenicians, and the ADONIS and APOLLO of the Greeks, were all forms of the sun. These gods represented the renewing power of life, the energy that keeps the world alive and refreshed."

Throughout ancient times, people built altars, temples, and mounds to honor the sun. Many of these sacred places still stand today, including the pyramids of Yucatan and Egypt, the snake mounds of the American Indians, the Zikkurats of Babylon and Chaldea, the round towers of Ireland, and the great stone circles in Britain and Normandy. Even the Tower of Babel, which the Bible says was built to reach God, may have actually been an observatory to study the stars.

Both pagan and early Christian priests and prophets knew a lot about astronomy and astrology. Their teachings often make more sense when viewed through the lens of these ancient sciences. As people learned more about the movements and patterns of the stars and planets, they began incorporating astronomical ideas into their religious beliefs. Gods were given homes among the stars, with different planets being named after these deities. The fixed stars were arranged into constellations, and the sun and planets were believed to travel through these constellations, along with the moons that orbited some of the planets.

...

# The Solar Trinity

The sun, as the most important of the heavenly bodies visible to ancient astronomers, was linked to the highest gods and became a symbol of the supreme authority of the Creator Himself. From reflecting on the sun's powers and qualities, the idea of the Trinity, as we understand it today, was born. The concept of a Triune God is not unique to Christian or Jewish beliefs but appears in many of the world's great religions, both ancient and modern. The Persians, Hindus, Babylonians, and Egyptians all had their own versions of the Trinity. In each case, the Trinity represented three aspects of one Supreme Intelligence. In modern Masonry, God is represented by an equilateral triangle, with each side symbolizing one of the primary aspects of the Eternal Being, who is also shown as a small flame, called Yod (ʼ) by the Hebrews. Jakob Böhme, a German mystic, referred to the Trinity as "The Three Witnesses," saying that through these three aspects, the invisible divine becomes known in the physical world.

The idea of the Trinity is easy to understand when we observe the daily journey of the sun. Since the sun symbolizes all light, it has three distinct stages: rising, midday, and setting. Philosophers saw these phases as representing the three stages of life: growth, maturity, and decline. Between the soft light of morning and evening lies the brilliant peak of midday. God the Father, the Creator, is represented by the sunrise, and His color is blue, like the morning sky veiled in mist. God the Son, the radiant one who reveals His Father's glory to the world, is represented by the midday sun, shining brightly like a lion with golden hair. His color is yellow, and His power is eternal. God the Holy Ghost corresponds to sunset, when the sun rests briefly on the horizon, clothed in fiery red, before disappearing into the night. This symbolizes the soul's journey into darkness, only to rise again with the dawn.

For the Egyptians, the sun was a symbol of immortality because it dies each night but rises again every morning. Beyond its daily path, the sun also has an annual journey, moving through twelve sections of the sky called the zodiac, spending thirty days in each. Additionally, the sun follows a third path known as the precession of the equinoxes, slowly moving backward through the zodiac at a rate of one degree every seventy-two years.

Robert Hewitt Brown, a 32nd-degree Mason, explains the sun's yearly journey through the zodiac this way: "As the sun moves through the signs of the zodiac, it is said to take on the qualities of each sign or to triumph over it. In Taurus, the sun becomes a bull and was worshiped as Apis by the Egyptians and as Bel, Baal, or Bul by the Assyrians. In Leo, the sun becomes a lion-slayer like Hercules, and in Sagittarius, it takes the form of an archer. In Pisces, the sun appears as a fish—Dagon of the Philistines or Vishnu, the fish-god of the Hindus."

A close study of ancient religions shows that their priests served solar energy and that the highest god was often a personification of the sun. After thirty years of research into the origins of religion, Godfrey Higgins concluded that "All the gods of ancient times ultimately trace back to the solar fire, either as the god itself or as a symbol of a higher creative power."

Egyptian priests often wore lion skins during their ceremonies because the lion was a symbol of the sun. The sun is especially honored in the constellation of Leo, which it rules. At one point in history, Leo was considered the keystone of the heavens. Hercules, another solar figure, performed twelve heroic tasks, just as the sun completes twelve essential tasks during its journey through the zodiac each year. Like the Egyptian priests, Hercules wore a lion's skin as a belt. Samson, the Hebrew hero, also symbolizes the sun. His name reflects his solar nature, and his struggles with the Nubian lion and the Philistines (representing forces of darkness), as well as his feat of carrying away the gates of Gaza, all reflect aspects of the sun's journey and power.

Many ancient cultures had more than one sun god, with different gods and goddesses reflecting parts of the sun's energy. The gold decorations used by priests in various religions refer to solar energy, as do the crowns of kings. Ancient crowns often had pointed rays extending outward to resemble the sun, though later designs either bent these points inward or gathered them at the top under a globe or cross. Many ancient prophets, philosophers, and leaders carried scepters with the sun symbol at the top, surrounded by rays. All earthly kingdoms were seen as reflections of the heavenly kingdom, with the sun as the supreme ruler, the planets as his council, and all of nature as his subjects.

Many gods have been linked to the sun. The Greeks believed that Apollo, Bacchus, Dionysos, Sabazius, Hercules, Jason, Ulysses, Zeus, Uranus, and Vulcan either embodied visible or hidden aspects of the sun. In Norse mythology, Balder the Beautiful was seen as a sun god, and Odin was also connected to the sun, especially because of his single eye. In Egypt, deities like Osiris, Ra, Anubis, Hermes, and the mysterious Ammon shared similarities with the sun. Isis was considered the mother of the sun, and even Typhon, known as the Destroyer, was thought to be a form of solar energy. The Egyptian sun myth eventually centered around a mysterious god named Serapis. The Central American gods Tezcatlipoca and Quetzalcoatl, while mainly associated with the winds, were also linked to the sun.

In Freemasonry, the sun holds deep symbolic meaning. One of the sun's representations is Solomon, whose name, SOL-OM-ON, translates to "Supreme Light" in three different languages. Hiram Abiff, also known as CHiram by the Chaldeans, is another figure connected to the sun. His story, including his attack and death at the hands of the Ruffians, contains solar symbolism, which is explored further in *The Hiramic Legend*.

George Oliver, D.D., provides a clear example of the role the sun plays in Freemasonry's symbols and rituals in his *Dictionary of Symbolical Masonry*. He writes: "The sun rises in the east, and the east is where the Worshipful Master stands. Just as the sun is the source of all light and warmth, the Worshipful Master must inspire and energize the brethren in their work. For the ancient Egyptians, the sun was a symbol of divine providence."

The priests in ancient mysteries wore many symbols representing solar power. The gold sunbursts embroidered on the robes of Catholic priests today reflect this same idea, showing that the priest acts as a messenger of Sol Invictus, the Unconquered Sun.

...

# Christianity And The Sun

For reasons they believed to be necessary, those who recorded the life of Jesus chose to portray him as a solar deity. The historical figure of Jesus faded into the background, and almost all the important events described in the four Gospels align with the movements, phases, or functions of the celestial bodies.

Among the many stories Christianity borrowed from ancient pagan traditions is the tale of the beautiful, blue-eyed Sun God. His golden hair flows over his shoulders, and he is dressed entirely in pure white. In his arms, he holds the Lamb of God, symbolizing the spring equinox. This radiant figure is a blend of Apollo, Osiris, Orpheus, Mithras, and Bacchus, as he shares qualities with each of these pagan gods.

Greek and Egyptian philosophers divided the sun's journey through the year into four parts, each represented by a different figure. At the winter solstice, the Sun God appears as a newborn baby, having mysteriously escaped the forces of darkness trying to destroy him during winter's cold. Since the sun is weak at this time of year, it is shown with no golden rays, or hair, except for a single thin strand symbolizing the survival of light through winter's darkness. Because the sun's birth happens in Capricorn, it was often depicted as being nursed by a goat.

By the spring equinox, the Sun God becomes a beautiful youth with golden hair falling in curls over his shoulders, his light shining across all of creation, as Schiller described. During the summer solstice, the sun is shown as a strong, bearded man in the prime of life, representing the peak of nature's strength and fertility. By the autumn equinox, the sun appears as an old man with bent posture and white hair, slowly fading into the darkness of winter. These four stages mark the sun's twelve-month journey, during which it triumphantly passes through the twelve zodiac signs. In autumn, the sun enters the house of Virgo, symbolized by Delilah in the story of Samson, where its rays are cut and it loses its power. In Masonic symbolism, the harsh winter months are represented by three figures who try to destroy the God of Light and Truth.

The arrival of the sun was celebrated with joy, while its departure was a time of sorrow and mourning. This brilliant and radiant sun, the true light "which lighteth every man who cometh into the world," was seen as the ultimate benefactor, the one who brought life to everything, fed the hungry, calmed storms, and rose from death to restore life. This Supreme Spirit of love for humanity and generosity is recognized by Christianity as Christ, the Redeemer of worlds, the Only Begotten of the Father, the Word made Flesh, and the Hope of Glory.

• • •

# The Birthday of The Sun

The pagans celebrated December 25th as the birth of the Solar Man. They rejoiced with feasts, processions, and offerings at temples. This marked the end of winter's darkness and the return of the sun's light to the Northern Hemisphere. It was believed that the old Sun God had destroyed the house of the Philistines (representing the forces of darkness) to make way for the new sun, born that day from the earth alongside symbolic creatures of the underworld.

An anonymous scholar from Balliol College, Oxford, explains in *Mankind: Their Origin and Destiny* that "The Romans also had a solar festival, celebrated with games in the circus, to honor the birth of the sun god. It took place eight days before the Kalends of January—December 25. Servius, in his commentary on the *Æneid* (Book 7, verse 720), mentions that the sun is considered 'new' on December 25. During the time of Leo I, some church leaders even stated that Christmas was made special less by the birth of Jesus and more by the return, or 'new birth,' of the sun." On the same day, the Romans celebrated the birth of the Invincible Sun (*Natalis Solis Invicti*), as shown in the Roman calendars from the reigns of Constantine and Julian. This title, 'Invictus,' was the same one the Persians gave to their god Mithra, whom they believed was born in a grotto. Christians later depicted Christ's birth in a stable in a similar way.

The same scholar also writes about the Catholic Feast of the Assumption and its link to astronomy. "Eight months after the sun god's birth, he moves into the eighth sign of the zodiac and absorbs the celestial Virgin into his light. She disappears in his glow and glory. This event, which occurs each year in mid-August, gave rise to a festival. In this festival, it is believed that the Virgin Mary leaves behind her earthly life to join her son in heaven. The ancient Roman calendar of Columella mentions the disappearance of the constellation Virgo around this time, stating that the sun enters Virgo thirteen days before the Kalends of September. The Catholic Church celebrates the Assumption, or the reunion of the Virgin with her Son, on this date. This feast was once called the 'Passage of the Virgin,' and ancient texts like the *Library of the Fathers* contain descriptions of it. The Greeks and Romans also marked the disappearance of Astraea, the Virgin goddess, on the same day."

This Virgin mother, who gives birth to the Sun God, reflects the ancient Egyptian goddess Isis. An inscription on the Temple of Sais honors Isis with the words, "The fruit I have brought forth is the sun." While early pagans connected the Virgin with the moon, they also understood her as a constellation. Most ancient cultures believed she was the mother of the sun, and although the moon couldn't hold this role, the sign of Virgo could. According to Albertus Magnus, "We know that the constellation of the Virgin rose on the horizon at the moment we mark as the birth of our Lord Jesus Christ."

Some Arabian and Persian astronomers called the three stars in Orion's belt the Magi, who traveled to honor the newborn Sun God. The same author from *Mankind: Their Origin and Destiny* adds: "At midnight, the constellation of the Stable and the Ass, located in Cancer, rises to the meridian. The ancients called this *Præsepe Jovis*. Meanwhile, the northern stars forming the Bear were known as Martha and Mary or the coffin of Lazarus." These examples show how much ancient pagan symbolism was carried into Christianity, even though the deeper meanings have been lost over time. The Christian Church continues to follow many of these ancient customs, often giving shallow explanations when asked about their origins, unaware that each religion builds on the secret teachings of the one that came before it.

•••

# The Three Suns

The ancient sages believed that, just like human nature, the sun could be divided into three different forms. Mystics taught that every solar system has three suns, which reflect the three main centers of life in a person. These are known as the three lights: the spiritual sun, the intellectual or soular sun, and the material sun. In Freemasonry, these are symbolized by three candles. The spiritual sun represents the power of God the Father, the soular sun carries the life of God the Son, and the material sun is the means through which God the Holy Spirit is revealed. Mystics also divided human nature into three parts: spirit, soul, and body. The physical body is sustained by the material sun, the spirit is enlightened by the spiritual sun, and the soul is redeemed through the true light of the soular sun. The alignment of these three suns in the sky was one explanation for why planetary orbits are elliptical instead of perfectly circular.

The pagan priests viewed the solar system as a Grand Man and compared its three main centers of energy to the human body's brain, heart, and reproductive system. In the story of Jesus' Transfiguration, there are three tabernacles: the largest in the center representing the heart, and smaller ones on either side representing the brain and the generative system. The idea of three suns may also be connected to a natural phenomenon that has been observed throughout history. In the fifty-first year after Christ, three suns were seen in the sky at once, and two suns appeared in both the sixty-sixth and sixty-ninth years. William Lilly recorded twenty similar sightings between 1156 and 1648.

Hermetists believed that, just as the physical sun is the greatest benefactor of the material world, there is also a spiritual sun that provides for the invisible and divine aspects of nature—both human and universal. Paracelsus, a great philosopher, wrote: "There is an earthly sun, which gives all heat, and anyone with sight can see it; even the blind can feel its warmth. There is also an Eternal Sun, the source of all wisdom. Those with awakened spiritual senses will see this sun and know it exists, but even those who have not yet reached spiritual awareness can still feel its power through their inner sense, called Intuition."

Some Rosicrucian scholars gave special names to the three forms of the sun. They called the spiritual sun Vulcan, the soular sun Christ, and the material sun Jehovah, the Demiurge of the Jews. In this context, Lucifer represents the intellectual mind without the guidance of the spiritual mind, making it the "false light." This false light is eventually overcome and transformed by the true light of the soul, referred to as the Second Logos or Christ. The secret process of turning the false, intellectual light into the enlightened mind of Christ is one of the core mysteries of alchemy, symbolized by the transformation of base metals into gold.

In *The Secret Symbols of The Rosicrucians*, Franz Hartmann describes the sun in alchemical terms as: "The symbol of Wisdom.

The center of power, the heart of all things. The sun is a source of energy and a storehouse of power. Every living being contains within itself a center of life that can grow into a sun. In the heart of one who is spiritually reborn, divine power, awakened by the Light of the Logos, grows into a sun that illuminates the mind." In a note, Hartmann adds: "The physical sun is the reflection of the invisible spiritual sun. The spiritual sun is to the realm of Spirit what the physical sun is to the realm of Matter, but the material sun draws its power from the spiritual one."

Most ancient religions agreed that the physical sun was not a true source of power but acted as a reflector. The sun was sometimes shown as a shield carried by a Sun God, such as Frey, the solar deity of Scandinavia. This physical sun reflected the light of the invisible spiritual sun, which was the real source of life, light, and truth. The physical universe is receptive, meaning it displays the results of hidden causes that come from the spiritual realm. In this way, the spiritual world is the realm of causes, the material world is the realm of effects, and the intellectual or soul world serves as the bridge between the two. Christ, representing the higher intellect and soul, acts as "the Mediator," saying: "No man cometh to the Father, but by me."

Just as the sun is central to the solar system, the spirit is central to the human body. A person's organs and functions are like planets orbiting this inner sun, depending on its energy for life. The spiritual power within humans is divided into three parts, known as the threefold human spirit. All three are radiant and transcendent, and together they form the Divinity within man.

The lower nature of man—his physical body, emotions, and mental faculties—reflects this inner Divinity and brings its light into the material world.

The three parts of man's lower nature are symbolized by an upright triangle, while his threefold spiritual nature is symbolized by an inverted triangle. When these two triangles come together to form a six-pointed star, they represent the unity of the spiritual and material worlds. This symbol, known as "the Star of David," "the Signet of Solomon," or "the Star of Zion," illustrates how humanity connects both Nature and Divinity.

A person's animal nature is connected to the earth, their divine nature to the heavens, and their human nature bridges the two as a mediator.

• • •

# The Celestial Inhabitants
# of The Sun

The Rosicrucians and the Illuminati described angels, archangels, and other celestial beings as small suns, acting as centers of radiant energy surrounded by streamers of a powerful force called Vril. These streaming forces are the source of the common belief that angels have wings. Instead of physical wings, these beings have corona-like fans of light that allow them to move through the subtle, non-physical realms.

True mystics agree that angels and archangels are not shaped like humans, as they are often portrayed. Human forms would be useless in the ethereal worlds where these beings exist. Scientists have long debated whether other planets, such as Mars, Jupiter, Uranus, and Neptune, could support life. Many argue that creatures with human-like bodies could not survive in these environments. However, this view overlooks Nature's law that life always adapts to its surroundings. Ancient thinkers believed that life originated from the sun and that all living things absorb solar energy to grow and later release it as plants and animals. One idea suggested that the sun acts as a parent to the planets, with each planet connected to the sun by invisible cords that provide life and nourishment.

Some secret groups have taught that the sun is inhabited by beings whose bodies are made of radiant spiritual energy, similar to the glowing substance of the sun itself. These beings are not harmed by the sun's intense heat because their bodies are perfectly in tune with the sun's powerful vibrations. They resemble small suns, usually a bit larger than a dinner plate, though some more powerful beings are much larger. Their color matches the golden-white light of the sun, and they emit four long streamers of Vril energy that are always in motion. These beings also pulse or ripple, which causes the streamers to vibrate.

The most powerful and radiant of these beings is the Archangel Michael. All the beings that live on the sun and share his qualities are known today by Christians as "archangels" or "spirits of the light."

•••

# The Sun in Alchemical Symbology

Gold is connected to the sun and is often thought of as sunlight in solid form. When alchemical writings mention gold, they could be referring to either the physical metal or the sun, which is the source and spirit of gold. Sulfur, with its fiery nature, was also associated with the sun.

Since gold symbolized the spirit and base metals represented a person's lower nature, some alchemists were known as "miners." They were shown with tools like picks and shovels, digging through the earth in search of precious metals—symbolizing the search for noble qualities buried under materialism and ignorance. The diamond, hidden within black carbon, reflected this idea. The Illuminati used the image of a pearl inside an oyster, lying deep in the sea, to represent spiritual power. In this way, a seeker of truth became like a pearl diver, diving into the ocean of material illusion to find wisdom, which initiates called "the Pearl of Great Price."

When alchemists said that every living and non-living thing in the universe held the seeds of gold, they meant that even a grain of sand had a spiritual essence because gold represented the spirit within all things. A Rosicrucian saying explains this idea: "A seed is useless and powerless unless it is placed in its proper matrix." Franz Hartmann added to this idea, saying: "A soul cannot grow or evolve without the right kind of body, because the physical body provides the materials needed for development." (See *In the Pronaos of the Temple of Wisdom.*)

The goal of alchemy was not to create something from nothing but to nurture the seeds that were already present. Alchemical processes did not generate gold from scratch but instead helped the hidden seeds of gold to grow and thrive. Everything that exists has a spirit—a seed of the divine within it. Regeneration is not about placing something new where it did not exist before. Instead, it is about unfolding the divine essence already present in a person so that this inner divinity can shine like the sun and illuminate everyone it touches.

• • •

# The Midnight Sun

Apuleius, describing his initiation, said: "At midnight I saw the sun shining with a splendid light." The idea of the midnight sun was part of the mysteries of alchemy. It symbolized the inner spirit within a person shining through the darkness of their physical body. It also referred to the spiritual sun in the solar system, which mystics could see just as clearly at midnight as at noon, as the material earth could not block the rays of this divine sun. Some believed that the mysterious lights illuminating the Egyptian temples during the night were reflections of the spiritual sun, gathered and projected by the magical abilities of the priests. The strange light seen ten miles underground by I-AM-THE-MAN in the Masonic allegory *Etidorhpa* (Aphrodite spelled backward) may also symbolize this mystical midnight sun from ancient rites.

Primitive ideas about the struggle between Good and Evil were often tied to the cycle of day and night. In the Middle Ages, black magic was practiced at night, and those who followed the Spirit of Evil were known as black magicians, while those who served the Spirit of Good were called white magicians. Black and white were linked to night and day, and many mythologies referred to the never-ending battle between light and darkness.

In Egyptian mythology, the demon Typhon was part crocodile and part hog, both animals known for their earthy, crude nature. From ancient times, living creatures have feared darkness, while only a few use it as cover for their activities—these animals were often linked with the Spirit of Evil. As a result, animals like cats, bats, toads, and owls became associated with witchcraft. In some parts of Europe, people still believe that black magicians take the form of wolves at night to roam and destroy, which led to the stories of werewolves.

Snakes, because they live underground, were also connected to the Spirit of Darkness. Since the conflict between Good and Evil revolves around the generative forces of Nature, winged serpents became symbols of the transformation of human instincts into higher, spiritual forces. The Egyptians often depicted the rays of the sun ending in human hands. Masons may find this symbolism connected to the "Paw of the Lion," a grip that symbolizes the power to raise things to life.

• • •

# Solar Colors

The idea of three primary and four secondary colors is only a surface-level understanding. Since ancient times, it has been known that there are seven primary colors, not three. However, the human eye can only clearly recognize three of them. While green can be created by mixing blue and yellow, there is also a pure green that exists on its own and is not a mixture. This becomes clear when the light spectrum is broken apart using a prism. Helmholtz discovered that the secondary colors in the spectrum cannot be separated into primary colors. For example, when orange light passes through a second prism, it does not split into red and yellow; it stays orange.

Colors like blue, yellow, and red symbolize consciousness, intelligence, and force. These meanings are reflected in their therapeutic effects: blue is calming and has electrical properties, yellow is energizing and refining, and red creates heat and excitement. Minerals and plants also affect people according to their colors. For instance, yellow flowers tend to produce medicines that have effects similar to yellow light or the musical note "mi." An orange flower, associated with orange light, corresponds to musical tones like "re" or the chord of "do" and "mi."

The ancients connected the human spirit with the color blue, the mind with yellow, and the body with red. Heaven was seen as blue, the earth as yellow, and the underworld—or hell—as red. The fiery imagery of the underworld represents the nature of its intense, destructive energy. In the Greek Mysteries, red symbolized the irrational side of human nature, tied to uncontrolled passions and desires. In India, some gods—often forms of Vishnu—are shown with blue skin to represent their divine nature, beyond the physical world. In esoteric teachings, blue is considered the true, sacred color of the sun, while the sun's yellowish-orange appearance results from its rays passing through the material world, which distorts their original color.

In the early Christian Church, colors held deep symbolic meanings, and strict rules guided their use. However, since the Middle Ages, these meanings have been largely forgotten as people began to use colors carelessly. In their original symbolism, white or silver represented life, purity, joy, and light; red stood for Christ's suffering, the blood of saints, divine love, and warfare; blue symbolized the heavenly realm and spiritual contemplation; yellow or gold signified glory, fertility, and goodness; green reflected youth, growth, and prosperity; violet conveyed humility, deep love, and sorrow; and black represented death, destruction, and humiliation. Early church art even used the colors of clothing and decorations to show if a saint had been martyred and the nature of the work they did to earn sainthood.

Beyond the colors visible in the spectrum, there are many more wavelengths of color that humans cannot see—some are too low, while others are too high to register with the human eye. It is staggering to consider how little humanity understands about these hidden aspects of light and space. Just as people once explored unknown continents, in the future, they will explore these unseen realms of light, color, sound, and consciousness, using tools specifically designed for that purpose.

## The Zodiac and Its Signs

It is difficult today to fully understand how deeply the study of the planets, stars, and constellations influenced the religions, philosophies, and sciences of ancient times. The Magi of Persia were called "Star Gazers" for good reason, and the Egyptians were highly regarded for their skill in calculating the movements and power of celestial bodies and how these influenced the destinies of both individuals and nations. Ancient astronomical observatories have been discovered all over the world, though modern archaeologists often do not understand the true purpose behind these structures. Although ancient astronomers did not have telescopes, they still made impressive calculations using instruments carved from granite or shaped from brass and copper. In India, similar instruments are still used today, showing a high level of accuracy. For example, the observatory in Jaipur, Rajputana, contains enormous stone sundials that remain functional. In Peking, China, there is a famous observatory with large bronze instruments, including a simple telescope made from a hollow tube without lenses.

The pagans believed the stars were living beings that could influence the fate of individuals, nations, and races. Even the early Jewish patriarchs thought that celestial bodies took part in human affairs. This belief is reflected in the Bible, such as in the Book of Judges: "They fought from heaven, even the stars in their courses fought against Sisera." The Chaldeans, Phoenicians, Egyptians, Persians, Hindus, and Chinese all had zodiacs with many similarities, and various experts credit each of these cultures with the origins of astrology and astronomy. The Central and North American Indians also developed their own understanding of the zodiac, although their signs and patterns differed in some ways from those used in the Eastern Hemisphere.

The word "zodiac" comes from the Greek word ζωδιακός (zodiakos), meaning "a circle of animals," or, as some believe, "little animals." This name was given by ancient astronomers to a band of fixed stars about sixteen degrees wide that appeared to encircle the earth. Robert Hewitt Brown, a 32nd-degree Mason, explains that the Greek word «zodiakos» comes from zo-on, which means "an animal." He also points out that the word is derived from ancient Egyptian roots: zo, meaning "life," and on, meaning "a being."

The Greeks, and later other cultures influenced by them, divided this zodiacal band into twelve sections, each one sixteen degrees wide and thirty degrees long. These sections were called the Houses of the Zodiac. The sun, during its yearly journey, passed through each of these houses in turn. Star groups within these sections were imagined to form creatures, many of which were part animal. Because of this, these star groups became known as the Constellations or Signs of the Zodiac.

A common theory about the origin of these zodiac signs suggests that shepherds, watching their flocks at night, entertained themselves by imagining the shapes of animals and birds among the stars. However, this theory seems unlikely unless the "shepherds" were actually the priest-shepherds of ancient times. It is also doubtful that the signs of the zodiac came directly from the star groups they now represent. It is more likely that the animals connected to the twelve houses are symbolic of the different qualities and strengths of the sun as it moves through each part of the zodiac.

Richard Payne Knight writes on this subject: "The symbolic meanings given to certain animals were based on specific qualities that these animals represented. These meanings were not difficult to discover, as they came naturally from the mind's way of thinking. However, the star groups named after these animals do not actually resemble them. These animals were chosen as symbols to represent certain parts of the sky, which were probably dedicated to personified qualities that the animals symbolized." (*The Symbolical Language of Ancient Art and Mythology.*)

Some experts believe that the zodiac originally had ten houses, or "solar mansions," instead of twelve. In ancient times, two different systems were used to measure months, years, and seasons—one based on the sun and the other on the moon. The solar year was made up of ten months, each lasting thirty-six days, plus five extra days dedicated to the gods. The lunar year had thirteen months of twenty-eight days, with one day left over. During that time, the solar zodiac was thought to have ten houses, each covering thirty-six degrees.

The first six signs in the twelve-sign zodiac were seen as favorable because the sun traveled through them while passing over the Northern Hemisphere, bringing warmth and light. The Persians believed that these six signs symbolized the 6,000 years during which Ahura-Mazda ruled the universe in peace and harmony. The remaining six signs were considered unfavorable since the sun traveled through them while in the Southern Hemisphere, bringing winter to the Greeks, Egyptians, and Persians. These six signs represented the 6,000 years of suffering and hardship caused by the Persian evil spirit, Ahriman, who tried to overthrow Ahura-Mazda.

Those who believe the zodiac originally had ten signs suggest that Libra (the Scales) was added later. They argue that Virgo and Scorpio were once a single sign that was divided to create Libra, establishing "the balance" between the northern and southern signs. (See *The Rosicrucians, Their Rites and Mysteries* by Hargrave Jennings.) On this subject, Isaac Myer wrote: "We think that the zodiacal constellations were originally ten, representing a great androgynous being or deity. Later, they were changed, splitting into Virgo and Scorpio, making eleven signs. From Scorpio, Libra—the Balance—was created, completing the current twelve-sign zodiac." (*The Qabbalah.*)

Each year, the sun completes a journey through the zodiac and returns to the same spot where it started at the spring equinox. However, the sun falls slightly behind its previous position every year. Each zodiac sign covers thirty degrees, and since the sun loses about one degree every seventy-two years, it takes around 2,160 years to move backward through one full sign. This gradual shift through all twelve signs of the zodiac takes about 25,920 years to complete, although experts sometimes disagree on the exact numbers. This backward motion is known as the precession of the equinoxes. In this long cycle, called the Great Solar or

Platonic Year, each constellation takes its turn occupying the position of the spring equinox for roughly 2,160 years before giving way to the previous sign.

Throughout history, people have symbolized the sun using the constellation it occupied during the spring equinox. For nearly 2,000 years, the sun has crossed the equator in the sign of Pisces (the Two Fishes) at the spring equinox. Before that, for about 2,160 years, it crossed in Aries (the Ram). Even earlier, the equinox was in Taurus (the Bull). The bull likely became associated with this constellation because ancient people used bulls to plow their fields, and this activity took place during the time when the sun entered Taurus.

Albert Pike describes how the Persians revered Taurus and used astrological symbols to reflect this respect: "In Zoroaster's cave of initiation, the Sun and Planets were depicted above, made from gems and gold, along with the zodiac. The Sun was shown rising from behind the Bull." In the constellation Taurus, there is also a star cluster known as the "Seven Sisters," or the Pleiades, which Freemasons refer to as the Seven Stars found at the top of the Sacred Ladder.

In ancient Egypt, during the period when the spring equinox was in Taurus, the Bull Apis was considered sacred to the Sun God. The Egyptians worshiped the Sun God through the bull, believing that the god's presence filled this constellation when the sun crossed into the Northern Hemisphere. This belief gave rise to the saying that the celestial Bull "broke the egg of the year with his horns."

Sampson Arnold Mackey, in his book *Mythological Astronomy of the Ancients Demonstrated*, makes two interesting observations about the bull in Egyptian symbolism. Mackey suggests that the movement of the earth, known as the shifting of the poles, has changed the positions of the equator and the zodiac. He believes that, originally, the zodiac was aligned at right angles to the equator, with the sign of Cancer positioned at the north pole and Capricorn at the south pole. Mackey thinks the Orphic symbol of the serpent coiled around the egg represents the motion of the sun under these conditions. He uses examples such as the Labyrinth of Crete, the word "Abraxas," and the magic formula "abracadabra" to support his theory. About "abracadabra," Mackey writes:

"But the gradual disappearance of the Bull is cleverly remembered in the vanishing series of letters, perfectly representing an important astronomical event. For ABRACADABRA means 'The Bull, the only Bull.' When broken down, the phrase reads: *Ab'r-achad-ab'ra*—'Ab'r,' meaning 'the Bull,' and 'achad,' meaning 'the only.' Achad is also a name for the Sun, given to it because it shines alone—it is the only star visible when it appears. The remaining 'ab'ra' completes the phrase: 'The Bull, the only Bull.' The way the letters are repeated, with one removed at each step until none remain, is a simple yet effective way of preserving the memory of this fact. The name of Sorapis, or Serapis, given to the Bull in this ritual confirms it beyond doubt. The word 'abracadabra' disappears in eleven decreasing stages, just like in the figure. Remarkably, a serpent with eleven coils wraps around a three-headed figure, placed beside Sorapis. The eleven coils form a triangle similar to the one created by the eleven diminishing lines of the word abracadabra."

Nearly every religion shows traces of astrology. The Old Testament, shaped by Egyptian culture, contains many astrological and astronomical symbols. Most of Greek and Roman mythology can be linked to groups of stars. Some scholars believe the original twenty-two letters of the Hebrew alphabet were inspired by star patterns, with stars forming consonants and planets or celestial lights serving as vowels. These combinations spelled out words, which, if read correctly, revealed future events.

The zodiac marks the path of the sun through the constellations, creating the changes in the seasons. Ancient calendars were based on the equinoxes and solstices, with the year starting at the spring equinox on March 21, when the sun crosses the equator going north. The summer solstice, marking the sun's most northerly point, was celebrated on June 21. After that, the sun began moving back toward the equator, crossing it again at the autumn equinox on September 21. The sun reached its southernmost point on December 21, the winter solstice.

Four zodiac signs are permanently associated with the equinoxes and solstices. Although the signs no longer align perfectly with their original constellations, modern astronomers still use them for calculations. The spring equinox is linked with Aries (the Ram), a fitting choice, as the Ram leads the zodiac. Long before Christianity, pagans revered this constellation. Godfrey Higgins writes: "This constellation was called the 'Lamb of God.' It was also known as the 'Savior' and believed to save humanity from sin. It was honored with the title 'Dominus,' or 'Lord,' and was called the 'Lamb of God which taketh away the sins of the world.' Devotees would repeat the words in prayer: 'O Lamb of God, that taketh away the sin of the world, have mercy upon us. Grant us

Thy peace.'" The Lamb of God refers to the sun, which is said to be reborn each year in the Northern Hemisphere when it enters Aries, though due to a shift in the zodiac, the sun now rises in Pisces.

The summer solstice is connected with Cancer (the Crab), which the Egyptians symbolized with the scarab beetle. This beetle was sacred in Egypt and represented eternal life. The crab fits the symbolism because, after passing through Cancer, the sun appears to move backward, retracing its path along the zodiac. Cancer also represents creation and birth, as it is ruled by the moon, the Mother of all life and the protector of nature's life forces. Diana, the Greek moon goddess, was known as the Mother of the World. Regarding the worship of feminine or maternal principles, Richard Payne Knight writes:

"By attracting and lifting the ocean's waters, the moon naturally seemed to rule over moisture. It was also believed to have a powerful effect on women's bodies, making it appear to govern nutrition and passive reproduction. Because of this, the moon was said to have received her nymphs—her helpers or symbolic forms—from the ocean. The moon was often symbolized by the sea crab, an animal that can shed injured limbs and regrow them. This regeneration connects the crab to the idea of life cycles, making it a fitting symbol for the maternal principle of Nature. For pagans, this maternal force was recognized as the origin of all life, and the moon became its natural home.

The autumn equinox takes place in the constellation of Libra (the Scales). At this point, the scales tip, and the sun begins its journey into winter. Libra was placed in the zodiac to represent the power of choice, allowing humans to weigh one option against another. Long ago, when the human race was still developing, people were like angels who did not know good or evil. They became aware of good and evil when the gods planted the seeds of mental awareness in them. Through their experiences, humans developed knowledge that not only restored them to their former state but also gave them unique individual intelligence. Paracelsus explained: 'The body comes from the elements, the soul from the stars, and the spirit from God. All that the mind understands comes from the stars—not the physical stars but the spiritual beings behind them.'

The winter solstice occurs in Capricorn, known as the House of Death. In winter, life in the Northern Hemisphere reaches its lowest point. Capricorn is depicted as a creature with the upper body of a goat and the tail of a fish. During this time, the sun's power is weakest, but after passing through Capricorn, the sun begins to grow stronger. In Greek mythology, it was said that Jupiter, the Sun God, was nursed by a goat. John Cole offers a different interpretation of Capricorn in *A Treatise on the Circular Zodiac of Tentyra, in Egypt*: 'The Goat rising from the fish symbolizes the rise of Babylon's towering buildings from the marshes. The two horns of the Goat represent the two cities, Nineveh and Babylon—one on the Tigris River and the other on the Euphrates—but both ruled by a single power.'

It takes about 2,160 years for the sun to move backward through one zodiac sign, a period known as an age. These ages are named after the sign the sun passes through at the spring equinox each year. This is why we refer to the Taurian Age, the Aryan Age, the Piscean Age, and the Aquarian Age. During each of these ages, religious worship reflects the qualities of the zodiac sign associated with it. The sun is believed to take on the personality of each sign, just as a spirit takes on a body. These twelve signs are like the jewels in the sun's breastplate, with its light shining through each one in turn.

This system helps explain why certain religious symbols appear during specific times in history. For example, during the Taurian Age, the sun was connected to Apis, the sacred bull, and the Bull became a symbol of Osiris. (For more details about how astrological ages relate to the Bible, see *The Message of the Stars* by Max and Augusta Foss Heindel.) During the Aryan Age, the Lamb became sacred, and priests were called shepherds. At this time, sheep and goats were sacrificed, and a scapegoat was chosen to carry away the sins of Israel.

In the Piscean Age, the Fish became the symbol of divinity. The Sun God is said to have fed the masses with two fish. In the frontispiece of *Ancient Faiths* by Inman, the goddess Isis is shown with a fish on her head. The Indian god Krishna, in one of his incarnations, was thrown from the mouth of a fish. Jesus is also called the Fisher of Men. John P. Lundy explains: 'The word Fish is an abbreviation for the full title, Jesus Christ, Son of God, Savior, and Cross. As St. Augustine said, "If you join together the first letters of the five Greek words, Ἰησοῦς Χριστός Θεοῦ Υἱός Σωτήρ (Jesus Christ, Son of God, Savior), they spell ΙΧΘΥΣ, which means Fish. In this word, Christ is symbolized because He was able to live in the depths of this world without sin.»' (*Monumental Christianity*). Many Christians honor Friday, a day sacred to the Virgin (Venus), by eating fish instead of meat.

The fish was one of the earliest symbols of Christianity, and when drawn in the sand, it served as a secret sign that identified one Christian to another.

Aquarius is known as the Sign of the Water Bearer, symbolized by the man carrying a jug of water mentioned in the New Testament. This figure is sometimes shown as an angelic being, thought to be androgynous, either pouring water from a vessel or carrying it on the shoulder. In some Eastern traditions, the water vessel alone is used as the symbol. Edward Upham, in *History and Doctrine of Buddhism*, describes Aquarius as a pot with a color between blue and yellow, calling it 'the single house of Saturn.'

When the planet Uranus was discovered by Herschel, the second half of Aquarius was assigned to it. The water flowing from Aquarius's urn is often called 'the waters of eternal life.' Like all zodiac signs, Aquarius represents one of the ways the sun shapes human worship of the divine."

There are two main systems of astrological philosophy. One is the Ptolemaic system, which is geocentric. In this view, the earth is considered the center of the solar system, with the sun, moon, and planets revolving around it. Though astronomically incorrect, the geocentric model has proven reliable when applied to the material nature of earthly things over thousands of years. A close study of the works of great occultists and their diagrams shows that many of them were familiar with another way of organizing the heavenly bodies.

The second system is called the heliocentric model, which places the sun at the center of the solar system, with the planets and their moons orbiting around it. However, since this system is relatively new, there hasn't yet been enough time to fully study or catalog how its aspects affect people and events. Geocentric astrology focuses on earthly concerns, while heliocentric astrology aims to understand higher intellectual and spiritual aspects of life.

An important detail to remember is that when ancient astrologers said the sun was in a particular zodiac sign, they meant that the sun was casting its light into that sign from the opposite one. For example, when the sun is said to be in Taurus, it is actually in the opposite sign, Scorpio, sending its rays toward Taurus. This difference led to two branches of philosophy: the geocentric, which is outward and material, and the heliocentric, which is inward and spiritual. While ordinary people worshipped the outward reflection of the sun in Taurus (symbolized by the Bull), the wise revered the sun's true position in Scorpio, represented by the Scorpion or the Serpent, symbols of hidden spiritual knowledge.

Scorpio has three symbols. The most common is the Scorpion, which the ancients called the "backbiter," symbolizing deceit and perversion. Another symbol is the Serpent, which represents wisdom. The rarest symbol is the Eagle, which reflects Scorpio's highest spiritual nature. While the stars in the Scorpio constellation resemble both a bird and a scorpion, the Eagle—known as the king of birds—symbolizes the highest potential of Scorpio, rising above the earthly nature of the scorpion. Since Taurus and Scorpio are opposite signs, their symbols are often connected. As E. M. Plunket explains in *Ancient Calendars and Constellations*: "The

Scorpion (Scorpio) joins Mithras in his battle with the Bull, and the spirits of the spring and autumn equinoxes are always present in both joyful and sorrowful forms."

The Egyptians, Assyrians, and Babylonians, who viewed the sun as a Bull, saw the zodiac as a series of furrows plowed by a celestial Ox dragging the sun behind it. This connection explains why people offered sacrifices of bulls and paraded decorated oxen through the streets, accompanied by temple priests, musicians, and dancers. However, the wisest among them, who wore the Serpent symbol of Scorpio (the Uræus) on their foreheads, did not participate in these rituals, seeing them as more appropriate for the general population.

The sun is often shown with its rays forming a shaggy mane, connecting it to the lion. Robert Hewitt Brown, a 32nd-degree Mason, explains the link between the constellation Leo and the summer solstice: "On June 21, when the sun reaches the summer solstice, the constellation Leo, only 30 degrees ahead, seems to lead the way, helping lift the sun to the top of the zodiac's arc. This connection between Leo and the sun's return to power explains why the ancients revered this constellation. Astrologers called Leo the 'sole house of the sun,' and taught that the world was created when the sun was in this sign. Both the Egyptians and Mexicans worshipped the lion. The chief Druid of Britain even held the title of Lion." (*Stellar Theology and Masonic Astronomy.*)

When the Aquarian Age fully begins, the sun will be in Leo, according to the distinction between geocentric and heliocentric astrology. At that time, secret spiritual traditions will once again include initiation rites known as the "Grip of the Lion's Paw," which symbolizes raising the soul to a higher state. (This will be like the story of Lazarus rising from the dead.)

The age of the zodiac is highly debated. It is a major mistake to say that it originated only a few thousand years before the Christian Era. The zodiac must be old enough to date back to a time when the signs and symbols perfectly matched the positions of the constellations, which reflected the sun's activity throughout each of the twelve months. One author, after years of study, believed the idea of the zodiac to be at least five million years old. It is likely that the knowledge of the zodiac came from ancient civilizations like Atlantis or Lemuria. About ten thousand years before the Christian Era, a destructive period began when knowledge was suppressed, and many records, monuments, and artifacts were destroyed. Only a few relics, such as copper knives, arrowheads, and cave carvings, remain as silent proof of those lost civilizations. Some massive structures, like the mysterious monoliths on Easter Island, also serve as evidence of lost knowledge, arts, and people. Humanity is incredibly old. Modern science measures human history in tens of thousands of years, but occult teachings believe it spans millions. There is an old saying that "Mother Earth has shaken many civilizations from her back," and it is reasonable to believe that astrology and astronomy may have existed millions of years before the first white man appeared.

The ancient occultists had a profound understanding of evolution. They saw all life as existing in different stages of growth. They believed that grains of sand were evolving into human consciousness (though not in physical form), that humans were becoming planets, that planets were becoming solar systems, and that solar systems were becoming cosmic chains. Each step in this process continued endlessly. At one stage between the formation of a solar system and a cosmic chain, the solar system transforms into a zodiac. The zodiac's houses, in turn, became the thrones of twelve celestial rulers, or in some cases, ten divine orders. Pythagoras taught that the number ten, which forms the basis of the decimal system, was the most perfect number. He symbolized it with the lesser tetractys—an arrangement of ten dots forming an upright triangle.

The early astronomers divided the zodiac into twelve houses and chose the three brightest stars in each constellation to serve as rulers of each house. They further divided each house into three sections, each containing ten degrees, which were called decans. Each decan was split in half, creating seventy-two smaller sections, each covering five degrees. The Hebrews assigned a celestial spirit or angel to each of these sections, and this system led to the Qabbalistic tradition of seventy-two sacred names. These names correspond to the seventy-two decorations—such as flowers, knobs, and almonds—on the seven-branched candlestick of the Tabernacle, and to the seventy-two representatives chosen from the Twelve Tribes of Israel.

The only two zodiac signs not mentioned earlier are Gemini and Sagittarius. Gemini is usually represented by two children, who, according to ancient myths, hatched from eggs—perhaps the same eggs that the Bull broke with its horns. The myths of Castor and Pollux, along with Romulus and Remus, may have evolved from the stories of these celestial twins. The symbol of Gemini has changed over time. The Arabians once used a peacock as its symbol. Two bright stars in the constellation of Gemini still bear the names Castor and Pollux. Gemini was also associated with phallic worship, and the two pillars or obelisks found in front of temples and churches carry the same symbolism as the twins.

Sagittarius is symbolized by a centaur—a creature with the body of a horse and the upper body of a human. The centaur is typically shown holding a bow and arrow, aiming into the stars. Sagittarius represents two ideas. First, it symbolizes the spiritual development of humanity, as the human form rises from the animal body. Second, it represents ambition and aspiration, since the centaur aims its arrow high into the sky, just as humans aim for higher goals beyond their current reach.

Albert Churchward, in *The Signs and Symbols of Primordial Man*, explains the importance of the zodiac in religious symbolism: "The division here [is] into twelve parts—the twelve signs of the zodiac, the twelve tribes of Israel, the twelve gates of heaven mentioned in Revelation, and the twelve portals in the Great Pyramid that must be passed through to reach the highest degree. Likewise, there are twelve Apostles in Christianity and twelve original and perfect points in Masonry."

The ancients believed that the idea of man being made in God's image should be taken literally. They thought of the universe as a vast organism similar to the human body, with every part of the cosmic structure reflected in humanity. One of the most valuable lessons given to new initiates was the "law of analogy," which taught that everything in the universe mirrors aspects of human nature. Because of this belief, studying the stars was considered sacred, as the movements of the celestial bodies were seen as the active presence of the Infinite Father.

The Pythagoreans were often unfairly criticized for spreading the idea of metempsychosis, the transmigration of souls. However, the version shared with the general public was meant to hide a deeper truth. Greek mystics believed that the spiritual part of a person came into material life from the Milky Way, which they called the "seed ground of souls." This descent happened through one of the twelve gates of the zodiac. Each soul was thought to take on the qualities of the zodiac sign it entered through. For example, a soul that entered through Aries was described as being born into the nature of a ram, while one that came through Taurus would carry the qualities of the celestial bull. In this way, all human souls were symbolized by the twelve creatures of the zodiac, each representing the traits needed to incarnate in the physical world.

This belief in transmigration didn't apply to the physical body but to the immaterial spirit that journeys among the stars, evolving by taking on the forms of the sacred zodiac animals over time.

In the *Third Book of the Mathesis* by Julius Firmicus Maternus, we find an account of how the heavenly bodies were aligned at the beginning of the material universe: "According to Æsculapius and Anubius—who received the secrets of astrology from the god Mercury—the cosmic arrangement at the moment of creation was as follows: The Sun was placed in the 15th degree of Leo, the Moon in the 15th degree of Cancer, Saturn in the 15th degree of Capricorn, Jupiter in the 15th degree of Sagittarius, Mars in the 15th degree of Scorpio, Venus in the 15th degree of Libra, Mercury in the 15th degree of Virgo, and the Horoscope was positioned in the 15th degree of Cancer. Based on this arrangement, they believed that human destinies were aligned with these original positions, as detailed in the book by Æsculapius called Μυριογενεσις (which means 'Ten Thousand Births' or 'Countless Births'). According to this book, nothing in the destinies of individuals can conflict with the original structure of the universe."

The seven stages of human life are each guided by one of the planets. Infancy is ruled by the moon, childhood by Mercury, adolescence by Venus, maturity by the sun, middle age by Mars, old age by Jupiter, and the final stage of life—decrepitude and death—is governed by Saturn.

## The Bembine Table of Isis

A manuscript by Thomas Taylor includes this interesting statement: "Plato was initiated into the 'Greater Mysteries' when he was 49 years old. His initiation happened in one of the underground chambers of the Great Pyramid in Egypt. The ISIAC TABLE served as the altar where the wise Plato stood, receiving knowledge that was always within him, but the Mysteries awakened and brought it to life. After three days in the Great Hall, Plato met the Pyramid's Hierophant, a figure only seen by those who completed the three days, three levels, and three dimensions. The Hierophant gave Plato the highest spiritual teachings, each with its own special symbol. After staying three more months in the halls of the Pyramid, Plato was sent into the world to serve the Great Order, following in the footsteps of Pythagoras and Orpheus."

Before Rome was looted in 1527, no records mentioned the Mensa Isiaca (or Tablet of Isis). At that time, a locksmith or metalworker came into possession of the Tablet and sold it at a high price to Cardinal Bembo, a famous historian and antiquarian of the Republic of Venice, who later became the librarian of St. Mark's. After Bembo's death in 1547, the Tablet ended up with the House of Mantua, where it stayed in their museum until 1630, when soldiers under Ferdinand II captured the city. Many believed the soldiers destroyed the Tablet to collect the silver it contained, but this assumption was wrong. The Tablet was taken by Cardinal Pava, who gave it to the Duke of Savoy, who later presented it to the King of Sardinia. When France conquered Italy in 1797, the Tablet was moved to Paris. In 1809, Alexandre Lenoir mentioned it in his writings, saying it was on display at the Bibliothèque Nationale. After peace was restored, the Tablet was returned to Italy. Karl Baedeker, in his *Guide to Northern Italy*, noted that the Tablet was placed in the middle of Gallery 2 in the Museum of Antiquities in Turin.

In 1559, Æneas Vicus of Parma made a precise replica of the original Tablet, and the Chancellor of the Duke of Bavaria gifted one of these copies to the Museum of Hieroglyphics. Athanasius Kircher described the Tablet as "five palms long and four wide." W. Wynn Westcott stated its dimensions as 50 by 30 inches. The Tablet was made of bronze, decorated with enamel and silver inlays. Fosbroke adds: "The figures are engraved shallowly, and silver threads outline most of them. The bases where the figures sit or recline, which are left blank in prints, were originally made of silver and later torn away" (see *Encyclopædia of Antiquities*).

Those who know the basics of Hermetic philosophy will recognize the Mensa Isiaca as a key to Chaldean, Egyptian, and Greek theology. Father Montfaucon, a knowledgeable Benedictine, admitted that he could not fully understand the Tablet's symbols.

He even doubted the symbols had any real meaning and criticized Kircher for making things more confusing than the Tablet itself. Laurentius Pignorius published an essay in 1605 with a reproduction of the Tablet, but his cautious explanations showed he didn't truly grasp the meaning behind the symbols.

In 1654, Kircher tackled the mystery in his *Œdipus Ægyptiacus*. After years of research into ancient secret teachings, and with help from other scholars, he made significant progress in understanding the Tablet. However, the ultimate secret still eluded him, as noted by Eliphas Levi in his *History of Magic*. Levi wrote: "The learned Jesuit guessed that the Tablet contained the key to sacred alphabets, but he couldn't fully explain it. The Tablet is divided into three parts: at the top are the twelve houses of heaven, at the bottom are the different types of work done throughout the year, and in the middle are twenty-one sacred signs representing letters of the alphabet. At the center is a seated figure of the pantomorphic IYNX, a symbol of universal existence, similar to the Hebrew letter Yod, which all other letters evolved from. Surrounding the IYNX is the Ophite triad, matching the Three Mother Letters in Egyptian and Hebrew alphabets. To the right are the Ibimorphic and Serapian triads; to the left are the Nepthys and Hecate triads, which represent opposites such as action and rest, solid and changeable, fire that gives life, and water that creates growth. When these triads join with the center, they form groups of seven. A group of seven also lies at the center. These three groups of seven represent the complete structure of the three worlds and the original alphabet's letters, with one extra sign added, like a zero following the digits one through nine."

Levi's suggestion seems to imply that the twenty-one figures in the center of the Tablet represent the twenty-one major cards, or trumps, of the Tarot deck. If that's true, then perhaps the controversial zero card symbolizes the crown of the Supreme Mind. This crown might be shown by the hidden triad at the top of the throne in the middle of the Tablet. The first creation from this Supreme Mind could be represented by a magician or juggler, with symbols of the four lower worlds arranged on a table before him: a rod, a sword, a cup, and a coin. In this interpretation, the zero card stands apart from the others—it serves as the fourth-dimensional source from which all the other cards emerge and into which they ultimately combine. The circle or cipher on the card would support this idea since it symbolizes the higher realm that gives rise to the lower worlds, powers, and letters.

In 1887, Westcott gathered the few theories available from various scholars and published a rare book that gives the only detailed English description of the Isiac Tablet. This was the first proper English description since Humphreys translated Montfaucon's poor interpretation in 1721. While explaining why he avoided sharing what Levi seemed to believe should remain hidden, Westcott summarized his understanding of the Tablet: "Levi's diagram, which explains the Tablet's mystery, divides the Upper Region into the four seasons, each connected to three Zodiac signs. He also included the four-letter sacred name, the Tetragrammaton, linking Jod with Aquarius (also known as Canopus), He with Taurus (or Apis), Vau with Leo (or Momphta), and the final He with Typhon. This matches the Cherubic symbols: Man, Bull, Lion, and Eagle. The fourth symbol is either a Scorpion or an Eagle, depending on whether it represents good or bad intentions. In the Demotic Zodiac, a Snake takes the place of the Scorpion.

"In the Lower Region, he links the twelve simple Hebrew letters with the four parts of the horizon. See *Sepher Yetzirah*, chapter 5, section 1.

"The Central Region belongs to the powers of the Sun and the planets. In the middle, we see the Sun labeled as Ops, and below it lies a Solomon's Seal, positioned above a cross. This Seal is made of two overlapping triangles—one light and one dark—forming a complex symbol for Venus. Around the upright dark triangle, representing Fire, he placed the three dark planets: Venus, Mercury, and Mars. Around the inverted light triangle, representing Water, he placed the three light planets: Saturn, Luna, and Jupiter. Water, in turn, symbolizes female power, the passive principle, and figures like Binah and the Sephirotic Mother and Bride in the Kabbalah (see Mathers' *The Kabbalah*). Ancient planetary symbols contain a cross, a solar disc, and a crescent: Venus's symbol is a cross beneath a Sun disc; Mercury's is a disc with a crescent above and a cross below; Saturn's is a cross with its base touching the crescent's peak; and Jupiter's is a crescent connected to the left side of a cross. Each of these symbols holds deep meaning. Levi's original plate switched Serapis and Hecate but left Apis noir and Apis blanc unchanged—possibly because he associated Bes's head with Hecate.

"Having placed the twelve simple letters in the lower section, the seven double letters must align with the planetary region in the center. The great triad—A.M.S.—the three mother letters representing Air, Water, and Fire, surround the central Iynx or Yod. These are also connected to the Ophionian Triad: two Serpents and the Lion-like Sphinx. Levi's use of 'Ops' at the center refers to both the Roman goddess Ops, the spirit of the Earth, and the

Greek figure Rhea or Cybele, often depicted as a goddess riding in a lion-drawn chariot. Cybele is crowned with towers and holds a key." (See *The Isiac Tablet*.)

In 1809, Alexandre Lenoir published an essay in French about the Tablet. While the essay is creative and original, it adds little useful information. Lenoir argued that the Tablet was either an Egyptian calendar or an astrological chart. Most writers since 1651, including Montfaucon and Lenoir, either relied heavily on Kircher's work or were strongly influenced by him. A full translation of Kircher's original article—eighty pages of 17th-century Latin—has been made for this book. The double-page illustration at the beginning of this chapter is an exact reproduction of Kircher's engraving from the Museum of Hieroglyphics. The small letters and numbers on the figures were added by Kircher to help explain his commentary and will also be used here for clarity.

Like many ancient religious and philosophical artifacts, the Bembine Table of Isis has sparked much debate. In a footnote, A. E. Waite, unable to distinguish between the true nature and the supposed origin of the Tablet, echoed J.G. Wilkinson's views. Wilkinson, another respected scholar, claimed: "The original [Table] is extremely late and can roughly be called a forgery." On the other hand, Eduard Winkelmann, a scholar of great depth, defended the Tablet's authenticity and age. A careful study of the Mensa Isiaca reveals one key fact: even if the person who made the Tablet wasn't Egyptian, they were a highly advanced initiate with deep knowledge of Hermetic philosophy."

• • •

# Symbolism of The Bembine Table

This short explanation of the Bembine Table comes from Kircher's writings, with some added information from the Chaldean, Hebrew, Egyptian, and Greek mystical texts. The design of Egyptian temples was highly symbolic, with each room's layout, decorations, and tools holding deeper meanings, as seen in the hieroglyphics covering them. Next to the altar, which was usually in the center of each room, there was a pool filled with Nile water, which flowed in and out through hidden pipes. The temples also contained images of gods arranged in connected groups, along with magical inscriptions. These temples used symbols and hieroglyphics to teach new students the sacred knowledge of the priestly class.

The Tablet of Isis began as a table or altar, with symbols that priests used to teach secret knowledge. Different gods and goddesses had their own dedicated tables. The materials used for these tables varied depending on the importance of the deity. Tables for Jupiter and Apollo were made of gold, while those for Diana, Venus, and Juno were of silver. Other superior gods had marble tables, while lesser deities had tables made of wood. Tables were also crafted from metals linked to the planets associated with these gods. Just as a banquet table holds food for the body, these sacred altars held symbols that nourish a person's spiritual nature.

Kircher introduces the Tablet by saying: "It reveals the structure of the threefold world—archetypal, intellectual, and physical. The Supreme God is shown expanding from the center to the edge of a universe made of both living and non-living things, all energized by a single divine force called the Father Mind, represented by a three-part symbol. The Tablet also presents three groups of three from the Supreme One, each showing an aspect of the original three-part divinity. These groups are called the foundation of everything. The Tablet explains how divine beings assist the Father Mind in governing the universe. In the upper panel, we see the rulers of the worlds, with their fiery, airy, and physical symbols. In the lower panel, we find the Fathers of Fountains, who maintain the natural principles and laws. There are also gods of the celestial spheres and wandering spirits, shown as male and female figures facing their superior god."

The Mensa Isiaca is divided into three horizontal sections or panels, which may represent the layout of rooms where the Isiac Mysteries were taught. The middle panel is split into seven smaller sections, and the bottom panel has two gates, one on each side. The entire Tablet has forty-five important figures and many smaller symbols. These forty-five figures are arranged into fifteen groups of three, with four groups in the upper panel, seven in the middle, and four in the lower section.

Kircher describes these groups: "The figures differ in eight important ways: by their shape, position, gestures, actions, clothing, headwear, staffs, and the symbols around them—whether flowers, plants, letters, or animals." These eight ways of representing the figures' hidden powers are reminders of the eight spiritual senses that can help people understand their higher selves. Buddhists express this idea with a wheel that has eight spokes and follow the noble eightfold path to raise their consciousness. The decorative border around the three main panels is filled with symbols, including birds, animals, reptiles, humans, and mixed creatures. Some interpretations suggest this border represents the four elements, with the creatures symbolizing elemental beings. Others see the border as representing the archetypal realms, showing patterns of forms that later appear in the material world. The four flowers in the corners of the Tablet are sacred symbols because they always turn toward the sun, representing the part of human nature that seeks its Creator.

According to the Chaldeans' secret teachings, the universe is divided into four levels: archetypal, intellectual, sidereal, and elemental. Each level influences and reflects the others, with higher levels guiding lower ones, and lower levels responding to the higher. The archetypal level corresponds to the intellect of the Divine Trinity. In this eternal and spiritual realm, all lower forms of life—everything that exists, has existed, or will exist—are contained as original patterns or divine ideas. These archetypes are shown in the Tablet as a series of hidden symbols.

In the center section of the Table is the Spiritual Essence—a being that contains all forms and serves as the source of everything. From this essence come nine groups of energies, each forming a triad: the Ophionic, Ibimorphous, and Nephtæan Triads. This idea is like the Qabbalistic concept of the Sephiroth, where nine spheres emerge from Kether, the Crown. The twelve cosmic rulers—the Mendesian, Ammonian, Momphtæan, and Omphtæan Triads— are responsible for spreading creative forces and are shown in the upper section of the Table. These rulers act according to divine patterns formed in the highest sphere, where the archetypes reside. Archetypes are abstract forms in the Divine Mind that guide the actions of all lower beings.

In the lower part of the Table are the Father Fountains—four triads called the Horæan, Pandochæan, Thaustic, and Æluristic. These beings guard the great gates of the universe, ensuring that the influences from the higher rulers flow properly into the lower worlds. Egyptian teachings emphasize that goodness is the foundation of everything, present to some degree in all things. Everything strives for goodness because it is the source of all causes. Goodness spreads itself naturally, existing in all things, since nothing can give what it does not have. The Table shows that God exists within everything and that everything exists within God; it suggests that all parts are connected, and each reflects the whole. In the intellectual world, there are spiritual versions of everything found in the physical world, so the lowest things reflect the highest, and physical forms reveal spiritual truths. For this reason, Egyptians made images of material things to symbolize higher, invisible powers. They assigned the qualities of eternal gods to these material images to show that the physical world is just a reflection of divine reality. Everything in the hidden, spiritual realm becomes visible through nature.

The Archetypal and Creative Mind first expresses itself through the Paternal Foundation, and then through secondary gods called Intelligences. It spreads its power from the highest realms to the lowest in a continuous flow. Egyptians used the symbol of sperm to represent the spiritual spheres because each contains all the life that comes from it. Both the Chaldeans and Egyptians believed that every effect remains connected to its cause and constantly seeks to return to it, just as a lotus flower turns toward the sun. Through the Paternal Foundation, the Supreme Intellect created light first—the angelic world. From that light came the stars, and from the stars came the four elements and the physical world. In this way, everything exists within everything else, according to its nature. Physical elements are connected to the stars, just as the stars are connected to angels, and angels to God. Therefore, everything exists within the divine world, the angelic world, and the physical world all at once. Just as a seed contains a tree waiting to grow, the universe is God unfolding into physical form.

Proclus explains: "Every divine quality flows into all of creation and shares itself with all lower beings." One way the Supreme Mind expresses itself is through the power of reproduction, which it grants to all living things. Each being—whether a soul, a heavenly body, a plant, or a stone—reproduces according to its type, but all depend on the one creative power in the Supreme Mind. This life-giving force takes different forms depending on what it flows through. In minerals, it becomes physical existence; in plants, it creates life; and in animals, it produces awareness. It gives motion to the stars, thought to humans, intelligence to angels, and essence to God. All forms share the same substance, and all life draws from the same energy, existing together within the Supreme One.

Plato first introduced these ideas, and his student Aristotle explained them this way: "We believe this physical world is a reflection of another, greater world. If this world is alive, then the higher one must be even more alive. Beyond the stars, there are other heavens, more brilliant and immense than these, and they are not separated by space like the heavens we know. These higher realms are spiritual, not physical. There is also a kind of earth there, not made of lifeless matter, but filled with living creatures and natural things, just like here, but of a better kind. There are plants, rivers, and animals, but all of them are nobler than the ones we know. There is air full of eternal life. Although the life there is similar to ours, it is greater because it is unchanging, intellectual, and eternal. If someone asks how such things can exist without physical bodies, the answer is that they exist in a pure state, created directly by the First Cause without taking on material form. They are like mind and soul—they do not experience decay or destruction. Everything there is full of energy, strength, and joy, living a perfect life, all coming from one source and sharing the same nature. These beings are like perfect scents, sounds, colors, and tastes, each keeping its true form without mixing or corrupting each other. Unlike physical beings, they are simple and do not multiply but remain exactly as they are."

At the center of the Table is a large, covered throne with a seated female figure representing Isis, referred to here as the Pantomorphic IYNX. G.R.S. Mead defines the IYNX as "a transmitting intelligence," while others see it as a symbol of Universal Being. Above the goddess's head, the throne is topped with a triple crown, symbolizing the Triune Divinity—the three-part God known by the Egyptians as the Supreme Mind. This divine triad is described in the *Sepher ha Zohar* as "hidden and unknowable." In Qabbalism, the Tree of the Sephiroth is divided into two parts: the invisible upper part with three aspects and the visible lower part with seven. The three invisible Sephiroth are Kether (the Crown), Chochmah (Wisdom), and Binah (Understanding). These higher aspects are too abstract for humans to understand, but the seven lower spheres can be grasped by human thought. The seven triads in the central panel of the Table represent these lower Sephiroth, all coming from the hidden triple crown above the throne.

Kircher explains: "The throne shows how the three-part Supreme Mind spreads through the three worlds. From these three unseen realms comes the physical universe, which Plutarch called the 'House of Horns' and the Egyptians called the 'Great Gate of the Gods.' The top of the throne is surrounded by serpent-shaped flames, symbolizing that the Supreme Mind is full of eternal life and light, untouched by the physical world. The Table illustrates how the Divine Fire of the Supreme Mind reaches all creatures through the force of Nature, symbolized by the World Virgin, Isis, called here the IYNX, or the Universal Idea containing all forms." Plato used the word *Idea* to describe eternal forms that exist without matter. These immaterial forms serve as the patterns that the divine power used to shape the physical world.

Kircher describes the 21 figures in the central panel as seven key triads, each linked to a higher world. These triads originate from the invisible flame of the triple crown. The first is the Ophionic or IYNX Triad, which belongs to the fiery, intellectual realm called Aetherium. Zoroaster described this realm as ruled by strict forces. The second, called the Ibimorphous Triad, relates to the ethereal world of moisture. The third, the Nephtæan Triad, governs fertility. These three triads represent the intellectual and ethereal worlds connected to the Father Foundation.

The remaining four triads belong to the material worlds. Two of these triads relate to the heavens: the Osiris-Isis Triad, symbolized by two bulls (representing the Sun and Moon), and another pair of heavenly rulers. The other two triads are connected to the sublunary and underground realms: the Hecatine Triad and the Serapæan Triad. These complete the seven worlds governed by the Genii—the spiritual powers that rule the natural universe. Psellus quotes Zoroaster, saying: "The Egyptians and Chaldeans taught that there are seven physical worlds, governed by spiritual powers. The first is pure fire; the next three are ethereal; the final three are material. The last, called the terrestrial world, lies beneath the Moon and is full of darkness." Together with the invisible crown, these make up the eight worlds.

Plato believed that philosophers needed to understand how the seven circles under the first circle were arranged, according to the Egyptians. The first triad, connected to fire, represents life. The second triad, related to water, is ruled by the Ibimorphous gods. The third, linked to air, is governed by Nephta. From fire, the heavens were formed; from water, the earth; and air served as the mediator between them. The *Sepher Yetzirah* teaches that these three elements give rise to the seven directions: height, depth, east, west, north, south, and the Holy Temple at the center. The Holy Temple, shown as the great throne of Nature's spirit at the center of the Tablet, is the home of the seven powers that rule the world.

Psellus writes: "The Egyptians worshipped a triad of faith, truth, and love, along with seven fountains. The Sun, as the fountain of matter, rules over all; other fountains include those of the archangels, the senses, judgment, lightning, reflection, and mysterious characters." The Egyptians connected these fountains with specific planets. The Sun represents the solar world, the Moon governs the archangelic world, and Saturn rules the world of the senses. Jupiter is linked to judgment, Mars to lightning, Venus to reflection, and Mercury to the world of symbols. All of these meanings are reflected in the figures of the central panel of the Tablet.

The upper panel of the Table features the twelve signs of the zodiac, arranged into four groups of three. In each group, the central figure represents one of the four fixed zodiac signs: Aquarius (S), Taurus (Z), Leo (C), and Scorpio (G). These signs are known as the Fathers. In the secret teachings of the Far East, these four figures—the man, the bull, the lion, and the eagle—are called the winged globes or the four Maharajahs, who stand at the four corners of creation. The four cardinal signs—Capricorn (P), Aries (X), Cancer (B), and Libra (F)—are referred to as the Powers. The four mutable signs—Pisces (V), Gemini (A), Virgo (E), and Sagittarius (H)—are called the Minds of the Four Lords. This arrangement explains the meaning behind the winged globes in Egyptian symbolism. The four central figures (Aquarius, Taurus, Leo, and Scorpio, known as the Cherubim by Ezekiel) represent the globes, while the cardinal and mutable signs on either side form the wings. Thus, the twelve zodiac signs can be symbolized as four globes, each with two wings.

The Egyptians also depicted the celestial triads as a globe (the Father) with a serpent (the Mind) and wings (the Power) extending from it. These twelve forces shape the world and give rise to the microcosm, which represents both the twelve sacred animals in the universe and the twelve parts of the human body.

116

In an anatomical sense, the twelve figures in the upper panel can represent the twelve convolutions of the brain, while the twelve figures in the lower panel correspond to the zodiacal organs and members of the body. Each part of the human body is controlled by one of the twelve zodiac signs, demonstrating that humans are formed from these twelve sacred animals.

There is also a deeper meaning behind the relationship between the twelve figures in the upper and lower panels. This connection reveals one of the most hidden ancient secrets: the relationship between two zodiacs—the fixed zodiac and the movable zodiac. The fixed zodiac is described as a massive dodecahedron, with its twelve surfaces representing the outer boundaries of abstract space. From each surface, a great spiritual power flows inward, becoming one of the celestial hierarchies of the movable zodiac, which consists of stars that appear to move in the sky. Inside the movable zodiac, planetary and elemental bodies are located. The connection between these two zodiacs is reflected in the human respiratory system: the fixed zodiac represents the atmosphere, the movable zodiac represents the lungs, and the subzodiacal spheres correspond to the body. The energies of the twelve divine powers of the fixed zodiac are "inhaled" by the cosmic lungs (the movable zodiac) and distributed throughout the material universe. The cycle is completed when the lower world's negative energies are "exhaled" into the fixed zodiac, where they are purified by the divine nature of the twelve celestial hierarchies.

The Table can be interpreted in many ways. If the border of the Table is seen as the source of spiritual energy, then the throne in the center represents the physical body, with human nature seated on it. In this view, the entire Table symbolizes the aura around a person, with the border representing the outer shell of the auric field. If the throne symbolizes the spiritual realm, the border represents the elements, and the surrounding panels depict the different worlds or planes that come from the divine source. If the Table is viewed in physical terms, the throne represents the reproductive system, and the Table reveals the process of creation in the material world. From a physiological perspective, the central throne corresponds to the heart, the Ibimorphous Triad symbolizes the mind, the Nephtæan Triad represents the reproductive system, and the surrounding symbols represent the organs and body parts.

From an evolutionary perspective, the central gate represents both the entrance and exit point of existence. It also illustrates the process of initiation, where a person, after passing through various trials, reaches the presence of their own soul, which only they can fully understand. If we interpret the Table in terms of cosmogony, the central panel represents the spiritual realms, the upper panel symbolizes the intellectual worlds, and the lower panel corresponds to the physical worlds. The central panel can also represent the nine invisible worlds, with the figure labeled "T" representing physical nature—the footstool of Isis, the Spirit of Universal Life.

In alchemical terms, the central panel holds the metals, while the border represents the alchemical processes. The figure seated on the throne is the Universal Mercury, also called the "stone of the wise." The flaming canopy above the throne symbolizes Divine Sulfur, and the cube beneath it represents elemental salt.

The three triads in the central panel, also known as the Paternal Foundation, represent the Silent Watchers—the three hidden aspects of human nature. The two panels on either side symbolize the four lower aspects of human nature. There are 21 figures in the central panel, a number sacred to the sun, which consists of three primary powers, each with seven attributes. By Qabbalistic reduction, 21 becomes 3, symbolizing the Great Triad.

It is likely that the Table of Isis is connected to Egyptian Gnosticism. A Gnostic papyrus in the Bodleian Library refers to twelve Fathers, beneath whom are twelve Fountains (see *Egyptian Magic* by S.S.D.D.). The lower panel of the Table represents the underworld, emphasized by two gates: the great gate of the East and the great gate of the West. According to Chaldean theology, the sun rises and sets through these gates in the underworld, where it travels during the night. Plato, who studied for thirteen years under the Magi Patheneith, Ochoaps, Sechtnouphis, and Etymon of Sebbennithis, infused his philosophy with Egyptian and Chaldean teachings about triads. The Bembine Table visually represents Platonic philosophy, summarizing ancient teachings about the creation and structure of the universe. The best guide to understanding the Table is *Commentaries on the Theology of Plato* by Proclus. Additionally, many references to these principles can be found in the *Chaldean Oracles* of Zoroaster.

Hesiod's *Theogony* offers the most detailed account of the Greek creation myth. The Orphic version of the creation story has influenced many philosophies and religions, including Greek, Egyptian, and Syrian traditions. A key symbol in Orphic mythology is the cosmic egg, from which Phanes emerged into the light. Thomas Taylor explains that the Orphic egg corresponds to the mixture of limit and the limitless, as described by Plato in *Philebus*. Additionally, the egg is the third Intelligible Triad and represents the auric body of the Demiurge, or the creator god, who shapes the lower universe.

Eusebius, citing Porphyry, states that the Egyptians believed in a single intellectual creator of the world, whom they called Cneph. They depicted him as a figure with dark blue skin, holding a girdle and a scepter, wearing a crown with a feather, and shown with an egg emerging from his mouth. (See *An Analysis of the Egyptian Mythology*.) Although the Bembine Table is rectangular, it symbolizes the Orphic egg of the universe and everything within it. In esoteric teachings, the highest spiritual goal is to break the Orphic egg, which represents the spirit's return to Nirvana—the absolute state described by Eastern mystics.

In *The New Pantheon*, Samuel Boyse includes three illustrations of different parts of the Bembine Table. However, his work does not provide any significant new insights. In *The Mythology and Fables of the Ancients Explained from History*, the Abbé Banier discusses the Mensa Isiaca in detail. After examining the interpretations of Montfaucon, Kircher, and Pignorius, Banier concludes: "I believe it was a votive table, dedicated to Isis by a prince or private individual in gratitude for a favor they thought she granted them."

## Wonders of Antiquity

It was common for the ancient Egyptians, Greeks, and Romans to place lit lamps inside the tombs of their dead as offerings to the God of Death. Some believed that these lamps would help the deceased find their way through the afterlife. Over time, this tradition grew, and instead of only using real lamps, people began placing small terracotta models of lamps in the tombs. Some of these lamps were protected inside circular containers, and there are reports of finding the original oil perfectly preserved after more than 2,000 years. Evidence shows that many of these lamps were still burning when the tombs were sealed, and some claimed they were still burning when the tombs were opened centuries later.

The idea that ancient priests could create lamps with fuel that renewed itself as it burned caused much debate among medieval scholars. Some believed these lamps could burn for centuries, though only a few suggested they could burn forever. W. Wynn Westcott noted that more than 150 writers had discussed this topic, while H.P. Blavatsky counted 173. Some argued that the so-called everlasting lamps were tricks used by clever pagan priests, but many others believed the lamps were real. Some even thought the Devil himself created these lamps to deceive people and lead them astray from true faith.

Athanasius Kircher, a respected Jesuit scholar, offered different opinions on these lamps. In his book *Œdipus Ægyptiacus*, he suggested: "Not a few of these ever-burning lamps were the work of devils... All the lamps found in the tombs of pagans were placed there as part of false worship, not because they could burn forever, but likely because the Devil set them there to encourage belief in a false religion." Though Kircher acknowledged that some trusted scholars accepted the existence of these lamps, he later dismissed the whole idea as impossible, comparing it to myths about perpetual motion and the Philosopher's Stone.

However, he also presented another theory: "In Egypt, there are large deposits of asphalt and petroleum. What if these priests connected underground oil reserves to lamps with asbestos wicks through hidden pipes? How could such lamps not seem to burn forever?" Kircher believed this explained the mystery behind the so-called eternal lamps.

Montfaucon, in his *Antiquities*, agreed with Kircher's later conclusion. He thought that the stories of perpetual lamps in temples were based on clever mechanical tricks. He also noted that when some tombs were opened, smoke-like fumes sometimes escaped, making it seem as though something had been burning inside. When explorers later found lamps scattered on the ground, they assumed these were the source of the fumes.

There are many interesting stories about the discovery of ever-burning lamps in different parts of the world. One such tale comes from a tomb along the Appian Way, opened during the papacy of Paul III. Inside the sealed vault, explorers found a lamp still burning after nearly 1,600 years. According to a report by someone present at the time, the body of a young girl with long golden hair was found floating in a mysterious clear liquid, perfectly preserved, as if she had just died. The vault contained many objects, including several lamps, and one of these lamps was still lit. However, when the door was opened, the draft blew out the flame, and the lamp could not be relit.

Kircher included an inscription in his work, supposedly found in the tomb: "TULLIOLAE FILIAE MEAE" ("To my daughter Tulliola"). However, Montfaucon argued that this inscription never existed and added that, although there was no solid evidence, many believed the body found in the tomb belonged to Tulliola, the daughter of Cicero.

Ever-burning lamps have been discovered in many places across the world. Records from regions like the Mediterranean, India, Tibet, China, and South America tell of lamps that kept burning without needing any fuel. The following examples are selected from various discoveries made over the years.

Plutarch described a lamp that burned over the door of a temple to Jupiter Ammon, and the priests claimed it had remained alight for centuries without fuel. St. Augustine also mentioned a perpetual lamp in an Egyptian temple dedicated to Venus. He said that neither wind nor water could extinguish it, though he believed it was the work of the Devil. During the reign of Emperor Justinian, a lamp was discovered in Edessa or Antioch. It was placed in a niche above the city gate and protected from the weather. The date on the lamp showed that it had been burning for over 500 years before soldiers destroyed it.

In the early Middle Ages, a lamp was found in England that had been burning since the third century AD. The tomb it was found in was thought to belong to the father of Constantine the Great. Another example, the Lantern of Pallas, was discovered near Rome in 1401. It was found in the tomb of Pallas, the son of Evander, who was mentioned in Virgil's *Æneid*. The lamp, placed near the head of the body, had burned steadily for more than 2,000 years. In 1550, a marble vault was opened on the island of Nesis in the Bay of Naples. Inside, a lamp was still burning, though it had been placed there before the start of the Christian era.

Pausanias wrote about a beautiful golden lamp in the temple of Minerva that burned for an entire year without needing more fuel or even having the wick trimmed. Every year, they held a ceremony to refill the lamp, which also served as a way to mark the passage of time. According to the *Fama Fraternitatis*, when the tomb of Christian Rosencreutz was opened 120 years after his death, it was brightly lit by a perpetual lamp hanging from the ceiling.

Numa Pompilius, an ancient King of Rome and a powerful magician, was said to have caused an eternal light to burn in the dome of a temple he built in honor of a nature spirit. Another story tells of a mysterious tomb found in England with an automaton that moved when certain floor stones were stepped on. Since the Rosicrucian debate was popular at the time, many believed this tomb belonged to a Rosicrucian initiate. A farmer stumbled upon the tomb, which was brightly lit by a lamp hanging from the ceiling. As the farmer moved, his weight pressed the floor stones, triggering a mechanical figure in heavy armor. The figure stood, struck the lamp with an iron baton, and destroyed it, ensuring that the secret of the lamp's flame would never be discovered. How long the lamp had burned is unknown, but it was believed to have been many years.

There are also accounts of lights found in sealed tombs near Memphis and in Brahmin temples in India. However, these lights extinguished as soon as they were exposed to air, and their fuel evaporated. It is now believed that the wicks of these lamps were made from woven asbestos, which alchemists called "salamander's wool." The fuel was likely a product of alchemical experiments. Kircher once tried to extract oil from asbestos, believing that since asbestos was fireproof, the oil would provide an indestructible fuel. After two years of failed experiments, he concluded that the task was impossible.

Several ancient formulas for making the fuel of these lamps still exist. H.P. Blavatsky reprinted two of these recipes in *Isis Unveiled* from older works by Tritenheim and Bartolomeo Korndorf. One of these formulas will help give a basic understanding of the process:

"Sulphur. Burnt alum, 4 ounces; turn them into flowers until reduced to 2 ounces. To this, add 1 ounce of powdered Venetian borax. Pour highly purified spirit of wine over the mixture and let it soak. Then remove the liquid and pour in fresh spirit. Repeat this process until the sulphur melts like wax on a hot brass plate, without producing any smoke. This will serve as the fuel.

Now, prepare the wick in the following way: Gather fibers or threads of asbestos until you have a bundle as thick as your middle finger and as long as your little finger. Place these fibers in a Venetian glass, covering them with the purified sulphur mixture you prepared earlier. Set the glass in hot sand for twenty-four hours, keeping the heat high enough for the sulphur to bubble the entire time.

Once the wick is fully coated with the sulphur mixture, place it in a glass shaped like a scallop shell, making sure part of the wick stays above the surface of the prepared sulphur. Set the glass back on the hot sand and melt the sulphur until it grips the wick firmly.

When you light this lamp, it will burn with a steady, never-ending flame. You can place this lamp anywhere you like, and it will continue to burn without going out."

• • •

# The Greek Oracles

The worship of Apollo included the creation and upkeep of places where the gods could communicate with people and reveal the future to those worthy of such knowledge. Many ancient Greek stories tell of talking trees, rivers, statues, and caves inhabited by spirits like nymphs, dryads, or demons, who gave prophetic messages from these places. Some Christian writers claimed that these prophecies were tricks from the Devil to mislead people. However, they could not deny the reality of oracles since their own sacred texts referenced similar events. If the glowing onyx stones on the high priest's robe in Israel could show the will of Jehovah, then it was possible that a black dove, temporarily given the ability to speak, could deliver oracles in the temple of Jupiter Ammon. Similarly, if the witch of Endor could summon the spirit of Samuel to give Saul a prophecy, then a priestess of Apollo could call upon her god to predict Greece's future.

Among the most well-known ancient oracles were those of Delphi, Dodona, Trophonius, and Latona. The oracle of Dodona, with its talking oak trees, was the oldest. While the origins of oracular prophecy remain unclear, it is known that many caves and openings used as oracles were considered sacred even before Greek civilization developed.

The oracle of Apollo at Delphi is one of the ancient world's enduring mysteries. Alexander Wilder believed that the name Delphi came from *delphos*, meaning "womb," chosen because the cave and its vent resembled a womb. The original name of the oracle was Pytho, which came from the legend of the serpent Python. According to the story, the serpent emerged from the slime left behind by a great flood that wiped out humanity, except for Deucalion and Pyrrha. Apollo climbed Mount Parnassus, fought the serpent, and threw its body into the cave. From that point on, the Sun God, also known as the Pythian Apollo, gave prophecies from the cave. Apollo shared the honor of being Delphi's patron god with Dionysus.

Though defeated, the spirit of Python remained at Delphi to serve Apollo. The fumes rising from the cave were believed to come from Python's decaying body, and the priestess, known as the Pythoness or Pythia, inhaled these fumes to connect with Apollo. The Greeks believed Delphi was the navel of the world, symbolizing that the Earth was like a living being, and the connection between oracles and the navel held deep meaning in the ancient Mysteries.

The origin of the oracle is likely much older than the story of Apollo and Python suggests. The priests may have created this tale to explain the oracle's power to people they did not think deserved the real, hidden truth. Some say a priest from Hyperborea discovered the Delphic cave, but records show that the cave had been considered sacred for as long as history remembers. People traveled from all over Greece and nearby regions to ask the spirit inside the cave for guidance. The priests and priestesses guarded the cave closely, serving the spirit that gave prophecies to humanity.

The story of the oracle's discovery goes like this: Shepherds tending their flocks on Mount Parnassus noticed that their goats acted strangely when they wandered near a large crack on the mountain's side. The goats jumped and made odd noises unlike anything heard before. Curious, one shepherd approached the vent, which released strange fumes. As soon as he inhaled the vapors, he was overcome with a wild, prophetic excitement. He danced, sang, mumbled strange words, and began predicting future events. Others who approached the vent had the same experience. The fame of the place spread, and people came from far and wide to breathe the fumes and glimpse the future.

Some visitors could not control themselves, and, with the strength of madmen, broke free from those trying to hold them back. Many jumped into the vent and died. To prevent further accidents, a wall was built around the opening, and a prophetess was appointed to communicate with the oracle on behalf of those seeking answers. According to later stories, a golden tripod carved with images of Apollo as the serpent Python was placed over the vent. A specially designed seat was set on the tripod to help keep the priestess steady while she inhaled the vapors, preventing her from falling during her trance. Around this time, the story began to spread that the fumes came from the decaying body of Python, possibly revealed by the oracle itself.

In the beginning, young virgin maidens were chosen to serve the oracle. They were called Phœbades or Pythiæ and became part of the famous Pythian priesthood. It is likely that women were selected because their emotional and sensitive nature made them more responsive to the "fumes of enthusiasm." Three days before giving a prophecy, the priestess underwent a purification ritual. She bathed in the Castalian well, fasted, and drank only from the sacred Cassotis fountain, whose water was brought into the temple through hidden pipes. Before sitting on the tripod, she also chewed leaves from a sacred bay tree.

Some claim the water she drank was drugged to induce visions, or that the priests knew how to produce a gas that caused an intoxicating effect, which they channeled into the cave through underground pipes. However, neither theory has been proven, nor do they explain the remarkable accuracy of the oracle's predictions.

When the young prophetess completed her purification, she was dressed in sacred clothing and led to the tripod, where she sat surrounded by the fumes rising from the open fissure. As she inhaled the vapors, her behavior changed dramatically, as if another spirit had taken over her body. She began to struggle, tear at her clothes, and cry out in strange sounds. After a time, she grew calm, and an air of majesty seemed to come over her. Sitting stiffly with her eyes focused on a distant point, she began to deliver her prophecy. These prophecies were often spoken in hexameter verse, though the words were sometimes confusing or difficult to understand. Every movement she made and every sound she uttered was carefully recorded by five holy men, called the Hosii, who were lifelong scribes selected from the descendants of Deucalion.

Once the prophecy was given, the spirit left her, and the priestess began to struggle again. She was then carried to a room where she could rest until the intense state passed.

In his essay *The Mysteries*, Iamblichus explained how the spirit of the oracle—thought to be a fiery demon or Apollo himself—took control of the priestess: "Whether the prophetess receives the god's message through fiery vapors rising from the cave, or whether she becomes sacred to the god by sitting on the tripod, she fully surrenders to the divine spirit and is filled with the god's presence. When fire rises from the cave and surrounds her, she becomes illuminated by its brilliance. Sitting on the seat of the god, she aligns with his stable prophetic power. Through these two steps, she becomes entirely possessed by the god, who then speaks through her."

One of the most famous visitors to the Delphic oracle was Apollonius of Tyana, accompanied by his student Damis. After making offerings, Apollonius was crowned with a laurel wreath and given a branch of laurel to carry. He passed behind the statue of Apollo at the entrance of the cave and entered the sacred space. The priestess, also wearing a laurel crown with her head wrapped in white wool, gave him a prophecy. Apollonius asked if his name would be remembered by future generations. The priestess said it would, but it would be spoken of with slander.

Angered by her words, Apollonius left the cave. However, time proved the prophecy true, as early Christian writers labeled him the Antichrist. (For more on this story, see *Histoire de la Magie*.)

The priestess's messages were passed on to philosophers of the oracle, whose job was to interpret their meaning. These interpretations were then given to poets, who translated the messages into beautiful odes and songs, making them accessible to the public.

Snakes were an important part of the Delphic oracle. The base of the priestess's tripod was formed from the twisted bodies of three large serpents. Some sources say the young priestesses were made to stare into the eyes of a snake to enter a trance-like state, allowing them to speak with the god's voice.

In the early days, the Pythian priestesses were always young maidens, often in their teens. However, after a series of assaults on these young women, a new rule was made that only women over fifty could serve as the mouthpieces of the oracle. These older women dressed as young girls and followed the same rituals as the first priestesses.

Originally, the oracle gave prophecies only every seventh year on Apollo's birthday. But as more people came seeking answers, the priestess began delivering prophecies once a month. The exact times and questions for these consultations were decided by lottery or by a vote among the people of Delphi.

The influence of the Delphic oracle on Greek culture was immense. As James Gardner explained: "The oracle's words exposed many tyrants and predicted their downfall. It saved many lives and guided countless people along the right path. The oracle promoted useful institutions and encouraged progress. It supported moral virtue and helped advance civil liberty." (See *The Faiths of the World*.)

The oracle of Dodona was overseen by Jupiter, who gave prophecies through oak trees, birds, and brass vases. Many writers have noted the similarities between the rituals at Dodona and those of the Druid priests in Britain and Gaul. The famous oracular dove of Dodona would perch on the branches of the sacred oaks. There, it not only spoke in Greek about philosophy and religion but also answered questions from people who had traveled long distances to consult the oracle.

The "talking" trees stood together in a sacred grove. When the priests needed answers to important questions, they would undergo solemn purification rituals before entering the grove. There, they called upon the god believed to dwell within the trees. After the priests asked their questions, the trees responded with human voices, giving the answers they sought. Some say that only one tree, an oak or beech at the center of the grove, spoke. Since Jupiter was believed to reside within this tree, he was sometimes called Phegonæus, meaning "the one who lives in a beech tree."

One of the most fascinating parts of the Dodona oracle was the use of "talking" vases or kettles made of brass. These were so well-designed that, once struck, they would continue to ring for hours. Some accounts describe a row of these vases, which would vibrate in unison if one were struck, creating a loud, overwhelming noise. Other sources mention a large vase placed on a pillar, with a second column nearby holding a statue of a child with a whip. The whip had several cords tipped with small metal balls. As the wind blew through the open building, the balls would strike the vase, creating sound. The priests carefully listened to the number and strength of the impacts and interpreted the vibrations to deliver prophecies.

When the original priests of Dodona, called the Selloi, mysteriously disappeared, three priestesses took over the oracle's duties. These women interpreted the sounds from the vases and consulted the sacred trees at midnight. Visitors seeking the oracle's wisdom were required to bring offerings and make donations.

Another well-known oracle was the Cave of Trophonius, located on the side of a hill with an entrance so small that it seemed impossible for anyone to fit through it. After making an offering at the statue of Trophonius and putting on sacred clothing, the visitor climbed the hill to the cave, carrying a cake of honey. Sitting at the edge of the opening, the visitor lowered their feet into the cave. Suddenly, they were pulled entirely into the cavern, which those who entered described as being about the size of a large oven. After the oracle's message was delivered, the visitor was ejected from the cave, usually in a delirious state, with their feet coming out first.

Near the cave were two fountains that bubbled from the earth just a few feet apart. Those about to enter the cave drank from these fountains, each of which had unique properties. The first fountain contained the Water of Forgetfulness, which caused anyone who drank it to forget their earthly troubles. The second fountain held the sacred Water of Remembrance, known as the water of Mnemosyne. This water helped those who drank it remember the visions and experiences they had while inside the cave.

Though the entrance to the cave was marked by two brass obelisks, the cave itself, hidden behind a wall of white stones and surrounded by a grove of sacred trees, did not look particularly impressive. However, there is no doubt that those who entered the cave had strange and intense experiences. After leaving the cave, visitors were required to write down everything they saw and heard during their time in the oracle. The prophecies came in the form of dreams and visions, often accompanied by severe headaches. Some people never fully recovered from the effects of the delirium they experienced.

The priests interpreted the visitors' disjointed descriptions of their visions according to the specific question that had been asked. It is likely that the priests used some type of unknown herb to trigger the dreams or visions, but their ability to interpret these experiences was so precise it seemed almost supernatural. Before anyone could consult the oracle, they had to offer a ram as a sacrifice to the spirit of the cave. Using a form of divination called hieromancy, the priests determined whether the sacrifice was acceptable and if the time chosen for the consultation was favorable.

• • •

# The Seven Wonders
## of The World

Many sculptors and architects of the ancient world were initiates of the Mysteries, especially the Eleusinian rites. From the beginning of time, those who worked with stone and wood have belonged to a sacred order guided by divine inspiration. As civilization spread, cities were built and abandoned, monuments were raised to heroes now forgotten, and temples were constructed for gods whose broken statues lie buried in the ruins of the nations they once inspired. Research shows that the builders and sculptors of these ancient structures were not just skilled craftsmen but masters of their art, unmatched by anyone today. The advanced knowledge of mathematics and astronomy found in ancient architecture, along with the detailed understanding of anatomy displayed in Greek statues, proves that these artisans were brilliant minds, deeply educated in the secret wisdom of the Mysteries. This tradition led to the formation of the Guild of Builders, ancestors of the modern Freemasons. When building palaces, temples, or tombs, or crafting statues for the wealthy, these initiated artists embedded the secret teachings within their work. Even now, long after their bones have turned to dust, it is clear that these early craftsmen were worthy of the honors given to Master Masons.

The Seven Wonders of the World, though seemingly built for different purposes, were actually monuments designed to preserve the secrets of the Mysteries. Each was a symbolic structure placed in a specific location, and only those initiated into the Mysteries could fully understand their meaning. Eliphas Levi pointed out a connection between the Seven Wonders and the seven planets. These wonders were built by those known as Widow's sons in honor of the seven planetary spirits. Their symbolism is connected to the seven seals in the Book of Revelation and the seven churches of Asia.

1. The Colossus of Rhodes was a massive bronze statue, about 109 feet tall, and it took more than twelve years to complete. It was created by an initiated artist named Chares of Lindus. For centuries, people believed that the statue stood with one foot on each side of the harbor entrance, allowing ships to pass between its legs, though this theory has never been proven. Unfortunately, the statue stood for only 56 years before an earthquake destroyed it in 224 B.C. Its broken pieces lay scattered on the ground for over 900 years until they were sold to a Jewish merchant, who transported the metal on 700 camels. Some say the bronze was turned into weapons, while others believe it was used for drainage pipes. The statue, with its crown of sun rays and raised torch, symbolized the Sun Man of the Mysteries—the Universal Savior.

2. The architect Ctesiphon proposed a plan to the Ionian cities in the fifth century B.C. to build a monument in honor of the goddess Diana. Ephesus, a city south of Smyrna, was chosen as the site. The temple was made of marble, and its roof rested on 127 columns, each 60 feet tall and weighing more than 150 tons. The temple was destroyed in 356 B.C. by an act of black magic, though the blame was placed on a man named Herostratus, who was believed to be mentally disturbed. Although the temple was rebuilt, its original meaning was lost. The first temple was designed as a miniature version of the universe and dedicated to the moon, which represents the cycle of creation.

3. After being exiled from Athens, Phidias, the greatest Greek sculptor, went to Olympia in the province of Elis, where he created a colossal statue of Zeus, the king of the Greek gods. No detailed description of this masterpiece remains, though a few old coins provide some idea of how it looked. The statue's body was covered in ivory, and its robes were made of beaten gold. Zeus was said to hold a globe with a figure of the Goddess of Victory in one hand and a scepter with an eagle perched on top in the other. His head, crowned with an olive wreath, was bearded and archaic. The statue sat on a beautifully decorated throne. This monument was dedicated to the planet Jupiter, one of the seven great spirits who serve the Sun.

4. Eliphas Levi lists the Temple of Solomon as one of the Seven Wonders of the World, taking the place of the Pharos, or Lighthouse, of Alexandria. The Pharos was named after the island it stood on and was designed by Sostratus of

Cnidus during the reign of Ptolemy (283-247 B.C.). It was made of white marble and stood over 600 feet tall. Even in ancient times, its construction cost nearly a million dollars. Fires were lit at its top to guide ships at sea, and the light could be seen from miles away. An earthquake destroyed the lighthouse in the thirteenth century, though remnants of it were still visible until 1350 A.D. As the tallest of the Seven Wonders, it was associated with Saturn, the Father of the gods, symbolizing enlightenment for all humanity.

5. The Mausoleum at Halicarnassus was a grand structure built by Queen Artemisia in honor of her deceased husband, King Mausolus, whose name inspired the modern word "mausoleum." The building's design came from Satyrus and Pythis, and four renowned sculptors decorated the monument. It measured 114 feet in length and 92 feet in width and was divided into five main sections, representing the five human senses. At the top was a pyramid, symbolizing the spiritual side of humanity. The pyramid rose in 24 steps—a sacred number—and a statue of King Mausolus riding a chariot stood at its peak, with the figure measuring 9 feet 9½ inches in height. Although many attempts have been made to rebuild the mausoleum after it was destroyed by an earthquake, none have been fully successful. The monument was dedicated to the planet Mars and built by an initiate to spread wisdom to the world.

6. The Hanging Gardens of Babylon, also known as the Gardens of Semiramis, were located within the palace grounds of King Nebuchadnezzar, near the Euphrates River. These gardens were constructed in a series of terraces

that formed a pyramid, with a water reservoir at the top to irrigate the plants. Built around 600 B.C., the name of the designer has been lost to history. The gardens symbolized the different planes of the unseen world and were dedicated to Venus, the goddess of love and beauty.

7. The Great Pyramid was the most important of all the temples connected to the Mysteries. Its astronomical symbolism suggests it may have been built as far back as 70,000 years ago. It served as the tomb of Osiris and was believed to have been constructed by the gods themselves. The architect is thought to have been the immortal Hermes. The Great Pyramid symbolizes Mercury, the messenger of the gods, and it stands as a universal symbol of wisdom and knowledge.

## The Life and Philosophy of Pythagoras

While Mnesarchus, the father of Pythagoras, was visiting the city of Delphi on business, he and his wife, Parthenis, decided to ask the oracle whether it was safe for them to sail back to Syria. However, when the prophetess of Apollo sat on the golden tripod above the vent of the oracle, she didn't answer their question. Instead, she told Mnesarchus that his wife was expecting a son who would surpass all others in beauty and wisdom and greatly benefit humanity throughout his life. Mnesarchus was so moved by this prophecy that he changed his wife's name to Pythasis to honor the Pythian priestess. When the baby was born in Sidon, just as the oracle had predicted, they named him Pythagoras, believing he was destined for greatness.

Many strange stories surround Pythagoras's birth. Some say he wasn't just an ordinary human but a god in human form, sent to guide and teach humanity. Like other sages and saviors, his birth was said to be miraculous. Godfrey Higgins, in his *Anacalypsis*, draws parallels between Pythagoras and Jesus, noting that both were born in Syria—Pythagoras in Sidon and Jesus in Bethlehem. Both fathers were given prophecies about their sons being future benefactors to humanity. Both mothers were away from home when they gave birth: Mary had traveled to Bethlehem, and Pythagoras's parents had journeyed to Sidon for business. Higgins also notes that Pythasis, like Mary, had a spiritual encounter—hers was with a spirit of Apollo, who told her husband not to touch her during her pregnancy. Because of these similarities, Pythagoras was called a "son of God" and believed to be divinely inspired.

Pythagoras, one of the most influential philosophers, was born sometime between 600 and 590 B.C. He lived nearly 100 years, dedicating his life to the pursuit of wisdom. His teachings show that he was well-versed in both Eastern and Western esoteric traditions. Pythagoras traveled widely, learning from Jewish teachers about the secret traditions of Moses. The Essenes later focused on interpreting Pythagorean symbols. He was initiated into the Mysteries of Egypt, Babylon, and Chaldea. Although some say he studied under Zoroaster, it's uncertain whether his teacher was the same figure revered by the Parsees. Historians agree, however, that Pythagoras traveled extensively and studied with many masters.

After mastering the teachings of Greek philosophers and likely being initiated into the Eleusinian Mysteries, Pythagoras traveled to Egypt, where he faced many challenges before finally being initiated into the Mysteries of Isis by the priests of Thebes. From there, he journeyed to Phoenicia and Syria, where he was initiated into the Mysteries of Adonis. He then traveled to the Euphrates Valley to learn the secret knowledge of the Chaldeans near Babylon. His most important journey was to India, where he studied with the Brahmins of Elephanta and Ellora. According to *Ancient Freemasonry* by Frank C. Higgins, Pythagoras is still remembered in Brahmin records as Yavancharya, the Ionian Teacher.

Pythagoras is credited with being the first person to call himself a philosopher. Before him, wise men referred to themselves as sages, meaning "those who know." However, Pythagoras preferred the more humble term "philosopher," meaning "one who seeks wisdom."

When he returned from his travels, Pythagoras established a school in Crotona, a Dorian colony in southern Italy. Although people were initially suspicious of him, he soon earned the respect of leaders from neighboring colonies, who sought his advice on important matters. He gathered a small group of devoted students and taught them the secret knowledge he had gained, as well as the basics of occult mathematics, music, and astronomy—disciplines he believed formed the foundation of all arts and sciences.

At around sixty years old, Pythagoras married one of his disciples, a brilliant woman who gave him seven children. She not only inspired him during his life but also continued spreading his teachings after his death.

Like many great thinkers, Pythagoras's outspokenness earned him both political and personal enemies. One man, angry after being denied initiation into Pythagoras's school, sought revenge. He spread false information about Pythagoras, turning public opinion against him. Without warning, a group of attackers stormed the community where Pythagoras and his students lived, burning the buildings and killing the philosopher.

The stories about the death of Pythagoras differ. Some say he was killed along with his followers, while others claim that after escaping from Crotona with a small group, he and his disciples were trapped in a house that was later set on fire by his enemies. In one version, when the disciples realized they were trapped inside the burning building, they threw themselves into the flames, forming a bridge with their bodies so Pythagoras could escape. However, he is said to have died soon after, heartbroken over the failure of his efforts to enlighten humanity.

After his death, his disciples tried to keep his teachings alive, but they faced constant persecution. Today, only a little remains to honor the greatness of this philosopher. It is said that Pythagoras's followers never referred to him by name, instead calling him "The Master" or "That Man." This could be because the name Pythagoras was believed to contain a special arrangement of letters with sacred meaning. In *The Word* magazine, T. R. Prater wrote that Pythagoras initiated his students using a formula hidden within the letters of his name, which might explain why it was held in such high regard.

After Pythagoras's death, his school gradually fell apart, but those who had benefited from his teachings continued to honor his memory just as they had respected him during his life. Over time, Pythagoras was seen not just as a man but as a divine figure, and his scattered followers were united by their admiration for his extraordinary wisdom. In *Pythagoras and the Delphic Mysteries*, Edouard Schure tells a story that shows the strong bond among Pythagoras's disciples:

"One of the disciples fell ill and became poor. A kind innkeeper took care of him, and before the disciple died, he drew a mysterious symbol—most likely a pentagram—on the door of the inn. He told the innkeeper, 'Do not worry, one of my brothers will come to pay my debt.' A year later, a stranger passing by noticed the sign on the door. He told the innkeeper, 'I am a Pythagorean. One of my brothers died here. Tell me what I owe you for his debt.'"

Frank C. Higgins, in *Ancient Freemasonry*, gives a helpful summary of the teachings of Pythagoras:

"Pythagoras's teachings are of the greatest importance to Freemasons. His ideas reflect the combined wisdom of the leading philosophers of the ancient world and represent knowledge that everyone could agree on, free from controversy. His firm belief in the unity of God supports the idea that the supreme secret of ancient initiations was the oneness of God. The Pythagorean school functioned like a series of initiations. Students had to pass through several stages, and they were not allowed to meet Pythagoras in person until they reached the higher levels. According to his biographers, there were three degrees of initiation. The first was 'Mathematicus,' where students learned mathematics and geometry—subjects that formed the foundation of all knowledge. The second degree was 'Theoreticus,' which focused on practical applications of science. The third and final degree was 'Electus,' where students were fully illuminated and ready to absorb the deepest wisdom.

Students at the Pythagorean school were divided into two groups: the 'exoterici,' or those in the outer grades, and the 'esoterici,' who had passed the third degree and were entrusted with the secret teachings. Silence, secrecy, and absolute obedience were the core principles of this great order."

• • •

# The End

# Thank you for Reading

**You've Just Read a Piece of the Greatest Library Ever Rebuilt**

Thank you for reading.

This book is one of thousands we're restoring, reimagining, and translating as part of the **Modern Library of Alexandria** — a global movement to preserve and share humanity's most important ideas.

What was once lost to fire and time is now rising again — not just as memory, but as living, breathing knowledge, freely accessible to all.

**What You Can Do Next:**

- **Keep Reading.**

  Discover more legendary works — in beautiful print, audiobook, or digital form — at LibraryofAlexandria.com.

- **Build Your Own Library.**

  Every title is available as a paperback, hardcover, or collectible boxset — at true printing cost. Craft a personal library worthy of display.

- **Spread the Light.**

  Share this book. Tell others about the movement. Help us translate every timeless work into every language, so no reader is ever left behind.

By finishing this book, you've already taken part in something extraordinary.

**Join us at LibraryofAlexandria.com**

Together, we're rebuilding the greatest library the world has ever known.

With appreciation,
**The Modern Library of Alexandria Team**

**Visit:**

**www.libraryofalexandria.com**

**Or scan the code below:**